RTI* for the GIFTED STUDENT

S0-BCP-277

*RESPONSE TO INTERVENTION

TIER III

Independent Study

TIER II

Identified students are served according to their learning style with differentiated curriculum based upon the curriculum standards.

TIER I

Students are observed for the identification process. Use multiple measures, both qualitative and quantitative, to determine if modifications of the regular curriculum are required. Whole-class instruction is generally involved.

By Cecelia Boswell, Ed. D. and Vowery Dodd Carlile

DEDICATION

We would like to dedicate this book to Missy Mayfield and Shelby Waller for their work on *RTI for the Gifted Student*. They have listened, answered questions, and given us a shoulder to lean on when we needed it. Missy and Shelby have been valuable resources for us as we wrote *RTI for the Gifted Student*. Thanks to the both of you!

We would also like to thank our husbands, Kent and Gene, who have been patient with us as we spent hours on our computers instead of time with them.

Cecelia and Vowery

The purchase of this book entitles the individual teacher to reproduce copies of the student pages for use in his or her classroom exclusively. The reproduction of any part of the work for an entire school or school system or for commercial use is prohibited.

ISBN 978-1-56644-427-9
© 2010 Educational Impressions, Inc., Hawthorne, NJ

EDUCATIONAL IMPRESSIONS, INC.
Hawthorne, NJ 07507

Printed in the United States of America.

Table of Contents

About the Authors

Cecelia Boswell, Ed. D., is an educator who has more than thirty-five years experience in education. She has worked with children from kindergarten through grade twelve, as a teacher of migrant and gifted children and as a coach for competitive literary events. She has coordinated migrant, ESL, bilingual, and gifted education services. Dr. Boswell served as the Language Arts and Advanced Academics consultant for Education Service Center (ESC) Region 14 in Abilene, Texas, and as the state director for AP/IB Projects. Under her leadership, the Small Schools Guide for the Gifted, AP Task Force research, and twenty AP/IB Projects across the state were developed. Today, Dr. Boswell is an independent consultant and founder of Austin Creek Educational Systems. She is working throughout Texas with schools and ESC's, writing on-line courses and managing a variety of projects for Texas Education Agency, consulting for the Florida Department of Education, and conducting research for Texas International Baccalaureate Schools. She has just completed her term as president of the 3,000-member Texas Association for Gifted and Talented (TAGT) after serving as president-elect and for two terms as Region 14's representative on the State Board of Directors for TAGT.

Vowery Carlile is an educator with thirty years in the classroom. Twenty-one of those years has been in gifted education. Vowery is an author of forty teacher resource books and is also an educational consultant. She has worked on projects for the Texas Education Agency, such as the Small Schools Guide for the Gifted, The Fourth Grade Guide to Success for the Texas Performance Standards Project, a video for the Texas Performance Standards Project, and a PBS and TEA Awareness Campaign for Gifted Education. She also served as a pilot teacher for the Texas Performance Project. She was named Region 17's Teacher of the Gifted by the Texas Association for the Gifted and Talented in 2003. She has also served as the Region 17 representative on the State Board of Directors for TAGT. Today, Vowery is a full-time teacher of the gifted for grades K-12 in Sundown, Texas. She coaches four Destination Imagination© teams each year and serves on the Board of Directors for the Northwest Plains Destination Imagination Region. She also coordinates the Sundown Gifted Program. Vowery works as an educational consultant in the summer for school districts and Educational Service Centers throughout the state of Texas. She is the Region 17 Director of the Texas Performance Standards Project. She is now serving her second term as Region 17's representative on the State Board of Directors for TAGT.

Introduction

5

Introduction

RTI for the Gifted Student is written to update educators about the RTI process and how it applies to gifted/talented (G/T) learners. Included in this introduction is an overview of the following:

- Features of RTI for G/T students
- Value-added practice
- Comparison of RTI for G/T and for struggling learners
- Best practices of differentiation for G/T students
- RTI process for G/T students
- Characteristics of G/T students

Features of RTI for G/T Students

This book is built upon the best practices for the education of G/T students. Best practices include differentiation, research-based strategies, classroom management strategies, products, and product assessment.

In what ways does RTI for the gifted student look the same as or different from RTI for the struggling learner?

Features of RTI for the G/T parallel those for struggling learners in several ways. Both include…
- observation, identification, and documentation;
- research-based instruction based on student assessment and best practices;
- choice of activities based on pre-assessment of content;
- continuous monitoring of progress toward student self-assessment; and
- evaluation of process and products through rubrics with external and student self evaluation.

RTI for the gifted in a regular classroom is a process that evaluates students' reactions to appropriate curriculum. This appropriate curriculum includes research-based management and instructional strategies.

RTI for the gifted includes instruction to observe behaviors particular to gifted learners. These observations lead to screening and identification of G/T students for services.

RTI for the gifted services include both pre- and post-assessment with documentation to ensure student growth.

RTI for the gifted offers assessments that guide further educational decisions and opportunities for the gifted.

Value-added Practice

What is the Value-added practice provided in this book for G/T learners? The book…

- offers educators the freedom and understanding to differentiate for gifted learners;
- is built around best curricular practices that are research based;
- is steeped in instructional and classroom management strategies;
- creates a process that supports all students in the classroom while meeting the nature and needs of the gifted learner; and
- proposes avenues to identify students for G/T services through sound instruction and curriculum.

RTI for struggling learners includes the following four areas. Each one is defined as it applies to G/T education.

High-quality Instruction

States with a mandate for gifted education require specialized professional development for educators of the gifted.

Research-based Instruction

Standards for instruction of G/T are available through each state's Department of Education.

Screening and Identification

Multiple measures of qualitative and quantitative data are required for identification of G/T students for services.

Continuous Progress

G/T students must be monitored for continuous progress because state-mandated testing often provides a ceiling effect. Annual yearly progress (AYP) must be appropriate for this population.

Value-added practice for the gifted/talented population includes all requirements of RTI and includes research-based best practices for a G/T learner.

Comparison of RTI for
Struggling Learners and for Gifted Learners

The usual model for RTI is a 3-tiered triangle or pyramid. It works equally well for gifted learners as for struggling ones; however, the time spent in each of the levels should be inverted for gifted learners.*

Struggling Learners

Tiers and Best Practice
Struggling learners are provided interventions along with all students (Tier I). Armed with data that shows a lack of progress, the struggling learners are given intensive (30 minutes per day, 3 times a week) interventions (Tier II). When data indicates no progress with Tier II interventions, struggling learners are provided intensive instruction with new intervention strategies on a daily basis (Tier III).

No Child Left Behind (NCLB}
Same as the Gifted

Distinguishing Features
- A general education strategy to meet the needs of struggling learners early in their education

- A problem-finding and problem-solving method that informs decision makers of appropriate actions

- Interventions and progress are monitored continuously

- Decision about intervention strategies and Tier placement are determined by a team of professionals with data to support decisions.

The Gifted

Tiers
Gifted learners spend time with all students (Tier I), with other gifted students (Tier II), and doing independent study (Tier III).

Best Practice
The best practice selected contributes to student learning and continuous progress in response to both the particular and diverse needs of the learner.

No Child Left Behind (NCLB}
Although the strategies that guide the focus differ in goal, the focus is not different from that of special education:
- High-quality instruction

- Research-based instruction

- Screening and identification

- Continuous progress through product assessment

- Early intervention

- Progress monitoring during interventions

Distinguishing Features
- A general and specific education to address learners who struggle because their needs as a gifted learner are not met

- Based on best practices that include results to demonstrate learning

- Dependent upon progress monitoring through process observations and product evaluation

- Intervention plans designed for identification responses to best instructional practices

*Adapted from Casabarro, J. (2008). *RTI—Response-To-Intervention*. National Professional Resources, Inc. Port Chester, NY.

Best Practices of Differentiation for Gifted/Talented Learners

What is appropriate curriculum for gifted/talented learners? How does it differ from general education instruction? This book looks at best practices for the education of G/T students and includes research-based and classroom management strategies for implementation of those best practices. Best practices include, but are not limited to, the following:

Differentiation through Critical Thinking, Creative Thinking, Depth & Complexity, and Research & Independent Study

- Differentiation through Critical Thinking includes complex, abstract, and/or higher-level thinking skills. Focus is on relevant and open-ended tasks that develop research skills and methods. Critical thinking ensures basic skills are taught through complex thinking skills.

- Creative Thinking promotes the thinking process and product development that is based on the creation of unique ideas and that challenge current beliefs. Products must use new techniques, materials, and forms.

- Depth and Complexity is approached through definition supplied by Dr. Sandra Kaplan in a Jacob K. Javits project. The elements she describes are Language of the Discipline, Details, Trends, Patterns, Ethics, Unanswered Questions, Rules, Big Ideas, Across Disciplines, Changes Over Time, and Different Perspectives.

- Concept-based Differentiation supplies an overarching theme. It includes learning around a concept with a generalization that focuses the concept and creates a purpose for learning.

- Research/Independent Study offers differentiation of content that integrates multiple disciplines into self-selected work in an area of interest for the student. Differentiation through self-evaluation with rubric evaluations and other standardized instructions allow the student to grow intellectually and personally.

Differentiation with Research-Based Strategies

- Identifying Similarities & Differences (Comparing and Contrasting)
- Nonlinguistic Representations
- Cooperative Learning
- Generating and Testing Hypothesis

Differentiation with Instructional Management Strategies

- Curriculum Compacting
- Tiered Assignments
- Interest Centers/Interest Groups
- Learning Stations
- Agendas
- Exit Cards
- Learning Contracts

Best practices are presented with concrete examples for use in the RTI process for the G/T student. In addition, assessment and appropriate products to exemplify learning are also included.

Process

The process for identifying G/T learners is not as intensive as for struggling learners. In Texas the process in RTI is circumvented by the Texas State Plan for the Education of Gifted/Talented Students (State Plan), which requires local districts to determine methods of identification within parameters defined in the State Plan (www.ritter.tea.state.tx.us/gted).

Refer to your state's plan for specifics that move G/T learners through Tier I, Tier II, and Tier III. If your state does not mandate G/T education, the Texas State Plan is offered as a guide.

Tier I

Students are observed for learning characteristics and referred for the identification process. The district evaluates the student through multiple measures, both qualitative and quantitative, to determine if modification of the regular curriculum (state standards such as Texas Essential Knowledge and Skills [TEKS]) is required. Tier I instruction for G/T students generally involves whole-class instruction. See F-21 for a Tier I nomination form.

Tier II

When students are identified for services appropriate to their learning style, they are provided with differentiated curriculum in the regular classroom and/or in a resource class. Differentiation is based on the curriculum standards, but is at the pace, depth, and/or complexity that meets the specific learning needs of G/T students. Best practices as defined in this introduction and exemplified in this book are the basis for their differentiated learning, which provides intervention for the gifted students. See F-22 for an intervention form for Tier III.

Tier III

Tier III is designed for independent study. The Texas State Plan calls for G/T students to work with all students, to work with other G/T students, and to work alone. Tier III meets the requirement of working alone. Students must have the opportunity for independent study during the school year. For reference, see Texas Performance Standards Project and references in this book for specific means to address Tier III.

Tiers for struggling learners are inverted for the gifted/talented. The goal for struggling learners is to be integrated into the regular curriculum and classroom for all content areas, Tier I. The goal for gifted/talented learners is independent study, Tier III. As struggling learners move from Tier I to Tier II and/or III, their goal is to eventually move back down the pyramid to Tier I. G/T learners require appropriate learning opportunities in Tier I; Tier II is designed for cluster grouping of G/T students; and Tier III is designed for independent study.

RTI AND THE GIFTED CHILD

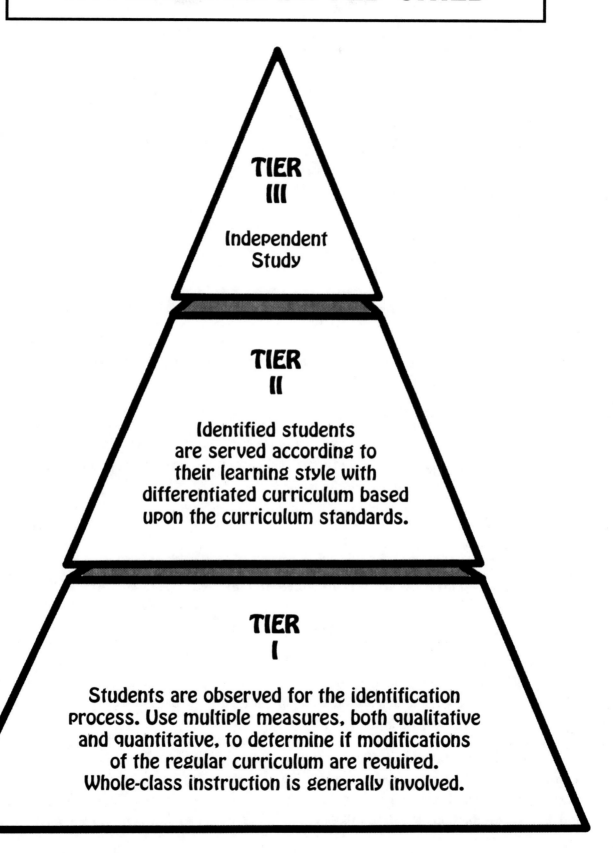

TIER III

Independent Study

TIER II

Identified students are served according to their learning style with differentiated curriculum based upon the curriculum standards.

TIER I

Students are observed for the identification process. Use multiple measures, both qualitative and quantitative, to determine if modifications of the regular curriculum are required. Whole-class instruction is generally involved.

Characteristics of G/T Students

There are as many lists of characteristics of G/T students as there are researchers in this field. The following abbreviated list covers the most pronounced characteristics. (For further insight, go to www.nagc.org or www.hoagiesgifted.org.)

- Learn more quickly
- Prefer company of adults or order youth
- More intense
- Sensitive
- Conceptual learners
- Analytical thinkers
- Insatiable curiosity
- Advanced language abilities in home language
- Sense of humor
- See ideas and problems from different points of view

Final Thoughts

The following are standard objectives for RTI:

- to continue to gather information and learn how to best meet the educational needs of the student;
- to solve the problem; and
- to determine the conditions that best enable the student to learn.

The next quote describes what has come to be called "Every Ed" as opposed to "Special Ed." These statements offer students opportunities to learn in the most appropriate environment with the most appropriate instructional strategies.

From No Child Left Behind:

> *"An LEA will provide training to enable teachers to teach and address the needs of students with different learning styles, particularly with disabilities, students with special learning needs (including students who are gifted and talented), and students with limited English proficiency; and to improve student behavior in the classroom and identify early and appropriate interventions to help these students."*

This quote states or implies that Response to Intervention is for all students, including gifted/talented students. Yet, when educators are queried about RTI, they often respond with the idea that this process is only for students with deficits in learning. This book targets practice for inclusion of the G/T student in any RTI effort.

Use this book to meet the needs of those learners who struggle in a different way. Gifted/Talented learners struggle against sameness, repetitive content and practice, and boredom borne from learning that is inappropriate in strategy and content. Recognition of G/T students' learning needs and styles with methods found in this book facilitate implementation of RTI for G/T.

Section I

Best Practices for Differentiation

- Critical Thinking
- Creative Thinking
- Depth and Complexity
- Concept-based Learning
- Critical Thinking
- Research/Independent Study

Best Practices for Intervention

Best Practices for Intervention to meet the cognitive abilities and the learning nature of gifted learners include, but are not limited to the following:

- Critical Thinking
- Creative Thinking
- Depth and Complexity
- Concept-based Learning
- Research and Independent Study

This section of *RTI for the Gifted Student* presents an overview of these intervention practices with examples of each.

Critical Thinking

Critical thinking involves a variety of skills. Richard Paul and Michael Scriven, noted researchers in the area of critical thinking, expressed the following at the National Council for Excellence in Critical Thinking in 1987:

> *"Critical thinking is the intellectually disciplined process of actively and skillfully conceptualizing, applying, analyzing, synthesizing, and/or evaluating information gathered from or generated by observation, experience, reflection, reasoning, or communication as a guide to belief and action."* *

Critical-thinking skills involve higher-order thinking, logical argument, and reasoning. The book will focus on…

- application, analysis, synthesis, and evaluation;
- reasoning abilities through logical thinking; and
- problem solving through problem-based learning.

*This statement was made by Michael Scriven & Richard Paul presented at the 8th Annual International Conference on Critical Thinking and Education Reform, Summer 1987.
Retrieved from http://www.criticalthinking.org/aboutCT/define_critical_thinking.cfm on September 29, 2009.

Bloom's Taxonomy*

When higher-order questioning is discussed, Bloom's taxonomy is often used as an example. Benjamin Bloom created a taxonomy for questions which include knowledge, comprehension, application, analysis, synthesis, and evaluation. The levels of application, analysis, synthesis, and evaluation will be discussed in this book and used in many intervention strategies for the gifted student.

Application involves applying the learned information in a new situation. Some verbs used with this level include *show, examine, complete, construct, illustrate,* and *solve.* Just because Bloom's taxonomy is often thought of in terms of questions, this does not mean that a question has to be used with the level. For instance, in a study of animals, a specific animal, its habitat requirements, and its survival needs are discussed. The students are then asked to utilize their learning about the animal to create a zoo habitat that would allow the animal to survive. Students must know the basics about the animal in order to create a home for it in the zoo. Students are still working at the application level even though instead of being required to answer a question, they must illustrate or show a zoo home for the animal.

Analysis is a way to see relationships among parts. *Compare/contrast, find* [similarities/differences], *categorize, examine,* and *identify* are a few verbs used with this level. An example of analysis would be to create a survey about a topic and display the results in a graph or chart. For instance, suppose a group of community members would like to have a walking track built in the city park. The track would cost several thousand dollars. In this process many community members would be surveyed about their feelings towards the track. The results of the survey and other information would be analyzed to help make a decision as to whether enough people would use the track to justify spending the money needed to build it. The decision will be based upon sound judgment.

Synthesis is the creation of something new by combining existing ideas or by finding alternate solutions to a problem. It can include putting parts together to form a new whole. Some verbs used with the synthesis level include d*evise, create, invent, plan, predict, imagine, propose, design,* and *compose.* An example of synthesis might include the design of a space station to be located on the moon. The station would require everything humans needed to survive.

Evaluation is the highest level of questioning. It involves making a judgment that is based upon all the information and defending it. Verbs that might be used with evaluation include *judge, select, choose, decide, verify, recommend, discuss, debate, justify,* and *determine.* An example of evaluation would be to judge the importance of sending more troops into the Middle East and to give reasons to support the judgment.

See E-1 for examples of questions and E-2 for question stems and activities that can be used for each of the top four levels of Bloom's Taxonomy.

Note: "E-__" refers to the Example Sheets found at the end of Sections I through IV and "F-__" refers to the Forms found in Section V.

*For information about the revised taxonomy, go to http://www.learningandteaching.info/learning/bloomtax.htm.

Logical Thinking and Problem Solving

Logical Thinking and Problem Solving are appropriate for Tiers I, II and III:

- **Tier I:** Use for observation of students who are using Logical Thinking and Problem Solving for characteristics of giftedness.
- **Tier II:** Students practice the processes of Logical Thinking and Problem Solving while meeting their learning and affective nature and needs.
- **Tier III:** Students integrate Logical Thinking and Problem Solving into research and independent study.

Logical Thinking

Students using logical thinking are given the opportunity to critically analyze ideas, information, and issues and to form opinions based on reasoned judgments. They use their imagination and creativity to express different perspectives, approaches, and ways of considering alternate possibilities. Students reflect on their learning and evaluate their thinking processes.

Logical thinking requires reasoning to be correct. Students look at the facts, string them together, and form a conclusion. The problem with this sequential thought process is that if there is an error in one fact, the conclusion produced may be false.

Most logical-thinking lessons involve deductive thinking. (See deductive thinking in Section III.)

Problem Solving

Problem solving as an intervention strategy involves overcoming obstacles that block the course to a solution. There are two types of problem solving: critical and creative. Both focus on an issue or problem, all possible factors for solutions, actually finding solutions, and, ultimately, finding the best solution.

The formal problem-solving process includes the following agreed-upon steps:

1. Define the problem.
2. Analyze the problem.
3. Generate possible solutions.
4. Analyze the solutions.
5. Select the best solution(s).
6. Plan the next course of action (next steps).

Problem-based Learning

Problem-based learning mirrors the problem-solving process, but with different descriptors. The process involves the following steps once the problem or issues has been defined (Paul 1992):

- Aim
- Facts
- Viewpoint
- Opinions
- Statement
- Concept and generalization
- Suppositions
- Consequences

The problem or issue may be one that the student selects or a scenario initiated by the teacher. The order of the process is not as important as the depth and breadth of thinking involved in the ideas submitted. The concept and generalization may be furnished initially by the teacher in order to guide students' thinking. After students have learned this process and can apply them naturally, they may assign their own concept and generalization as it applies to their problem or issue. Their personal development helps formulate their solution throughout the process. (See Section 1, Concept-Based Learning).

While it is best to begin with the aim and the facts, it is also important for students to determine the various viewpoints represented in the problem and the different opinions expressed, including those that are particular to the students. In the development of the statement, students ponder consequences and acknowledge suppositions. (See E-3 for examples. A blank reasoning model can be found in Section V, F-1.)

Creating Problem-based Learning Scenarios

Problem-based learning scenarios contain the following elements:

- Incomplete information
- Many possible ways to interpret the information given
- Students acting as professionals
- Multiple resources to approach
- Sense of urgency
- Connections among disciplines (e.g., science–math–social studies–language arts–society)

Examples in E-3 illustrate the development of a scenario and possible answers that could be found in a reasoning model.

Creative Thinking

As a curriculum framework for the gifted/talented program is developed, one of the pieces for intervention should involve opportunities for creative thinking.

When faced with problems or issues, the skills of creative/productive thinking encourages students to use a variety of approaches to problem solving, analyzing multiple viewpoints, adapting ideas and arriving at new solutions.

Creative thinking can be introduced, developed, or enriched through creative/productive thinking processes and creative problem solving. It is appropriate for Tiers I, II and III:

- **Tier I:** Use for observation of characteristics of giftedness.
- **Tier II:** Students practice the processes of Creative Thinking.
- **Tier III:** Students integrate Creative Thinking into research and independent study.

Creative/Productive Thinking Processes

Researchers define creative thinking through fluency, flexibility, originality, and elaboration.

Fluency asks students to produce many ideas or responses.
Examples:
List as many causes for the American Revolution that you can.

List as many articles of clothing as you can.

Flexibility asks students to analyze different points of view.

Examples:
Categorize the causes of the American Revolution that you listed above.

Look in/Think about your closet. How many categories of clothing can you find?

Originality asks students to produce unique responses.

Examples:
From the categorized class lists of causes of the American Revolution, select the ones that are unique among the others.

Invent a coding system or a space system for your clothes closet.

Elaboration asks students to incorporate details to an idea accurately and comprehensively in a way that enhances the outcome.
Examples:
Select one of the unique categories of the causes of the American Revolution. Elaborate on the category in order to explain your thinking to an audience of historians.

Describe the categories of your clothing for your school newspaper.

Creative Problem Solving

The most commonly accepted system for Creative Problem Solving is that of Parnes (1992). The steps include Fact, Problem, Idea, Solution, and Acceptance Finding.

Fact Finding

What are the facts discerned from the problem?
List facts according to WHO, WHAT, WHEN, WHERE, and WHY.

Problem Finding

Consider the problem in two or three ways. Decide what you believe the core problem to be.

Idea Finding

Using the problem statement, list as many solutions as possible (at least three).

Solution Finding

Determine the criteria to solve the problem. List each criterion in order of importance and weigh the solution against each. If the solution meets a majority of the criteria, it will likely be the solution that will produce the outcome you seek.

Acceptance Finding

Write the solution. Answer these questions relative to the solution:

- What steps are needed to take to solve the problem?
- What difficulties may be found?
- How can difficulties be overcome?
- Is there someone who can help?

If your solution does not provide the desired outcome, look at one of the alternative problems and repeat the process.

See E-4 for examples. F-2 provides a blank problem-solving form.

S•C•A•M•P•E•R Technique*

S•C•A•M•P•E•R is an intervention tool for generating new products and services. It consists of a checklist that helps students think of changes that can be made to an existing product or idea to create a new one. Using SCAMPER helps define possible new ideas. Many of the ideas may be impractical or may not suit the situation. However, some ideas could be good starting points for new ways of doing things. See E-5 for an example of the SCAMPER technique. A blank SCAMPER form can be found in Section V, F-3.

Here are the thought processes for which the acrostic SCAMPER stands:

Substitute

What can be used in the place of the product or a part of the product? What can you use instead of what is now used? A disposable camera is an example of a product that illustrates substitution.

Combine

Which parts or ideas can you combine? What could be added? How can you combine uses with something else? A clock radio is an example of combinations.

Adapt

What else is like this? How can it be adapted to fit another purpose? Hiking boots are an example of adaptations.

Minimize or Magnify

Minimize: Can it be smaller, lighter, less frequent, or divided? How? In what ways? I-phones demonstrate how objects can be minimized.

Magnify: Can it be stronger, larger, higher, or more frequent? How can it be made larger or stronger? What can be duplicated? Big-screen televisions illustrate products that have been magnified.

Put to Other Uses

Can it be used in a way other than how it was originally intended to be used? Drinking cups used as pen-and-pencil holders illustrate the idea of "put to other uses."

Eliminate

What can you take away or remove? What parts aren't really necessary? A cordless drill is an example of eliminating something.

Rearrange

Can parts be exchanged or the pattern changed? Can any components be interchanged? A 2-rotor helicopter is an example of a product that has been rearranged.

* Eberle, B. (1996). *SCAMPER*. Prufrock: Waco, TX.

Depth and Complexity

Content for gifted learners may be differentiated through the elements of depth, complexity, and pacing. This intervention strategy has layers (depth) and allows students to study content intricacies (complexity) in order to expand their understanding beyond boundaries.

- **Tier II:** Students practice with elements in content.
- **Tier III:** Students integrate elements into research and independent study.

The following categories used to define depth and complexity were developed by Dr. Sandra Kaplan, UCLA, for the Texas Education Agency through a federal Jacob K. Javits grant (www.ritter.tea.state.tx.us/gted). For the purpose of RTI for the gifted student, Dr. Kaplan's definitions and language are used and examples for each are provided.

Depth

Depth refers to the exploration of content within a discipline. Students *and* teachers dig more deeply into the curriculum. The deeper students delve into the content, the broader it becomes. Depth allows for exploration of the discipline by going past facts and concepts into generalizations, principles, theories, and laws.

Students investigate within a discipline utilizing Kaplan's elements of depth. Students…

- know and use the language of the discipline;
- use details to elaborate in the discipline;
- look for patterns in the discipline;
- look for trends in the discipline (forces that shape a body of knowledge);
- identify the unanswered questions of the discipline;
- identify and explain the rules or how information/events are organized in the discipline;
- are sensitive to the ethical considerations in the problem/issue/discipline; and
- look at big ideas that can be supported by the evidence from a body of knowledge.

See also Concept-based Learning on the following page.

Complexity

Complexity refers to the examination of a big idea, issue/problem, or topic for greater breadth of understanding. Complexity extends content in, between, and across disciplines. It helps us establish purpose and understand events, elements, and ideas that recur in order to predict and generalize between or among disciplines. See E-6 for examples.

Students investigate within a discipline utilizing Kaplan's elements of complexity. Students…

- look at ideas/information **over time**—past, present, and future;
- look at ideas/information **from different points of view;** and
- look for **connections** among/between ideas/information/disciplines.

Concept-based Learning

Brain research tells us that the human brain seeks patterns. The brain understands and organizes efficiently when it comprehends through categories the how and why of ideas and when it makes comparisons (Caine & Caine, 1991).

Concepts are pattern makers. They help the brain create systems of organization that promote thinking and information storage and retrieval.

An important irony of concept-based study is that while emphasis is placed on essential concepts and meanings, facts become more memorable than in a fact-based approach to learning. It is as though the concepts help learners build a series of shelves or cubicles into which they organize topical and factual data. (Tomlinson,1998).

Concept-based learning addresses the needs of the gifted learner. Students process information through a broad view—the big picture or concept. **Because of their capacity to see the whole before the parts, gifted learners learn best through concepts.**

What Is Concept-based Curriculum?

A concept is an idea that is timeless, abstract, and broad. Concepts focus the study of topics and integrate the curriculum. Skills are embedded in the study of a topic. An example follows:

TOPIC: Fairy Tales
CONCEPT: Patterns
Fairy Tales: Social Studies—Geography—Map skills
Fairy Tales: English-Language Arts (ELA)—Setting—Describe the setting and patterns of travel

Students study map skills (social studies) through fairy tales. Students find patterns of travel and describe the setting (ELA) in the fairy tales they study. They first describe the setting in narrative form and/or with graphics. From the patterns of travel they find, students apply map skills to develop of a map for the travels of the characters in one fairy tale they select.

A universal theme with generalizations serves as an organizing element. Selection of a theme that goes across the disciplines drives the curriculum.

Sample Universal Concepts That Can Serve to Organize Curriculum

Adaptation	Explorations	Order
Change	Forces	Patterns
Relationships	Conflict	Power
Community	Heroism	Structures
Interdependence	Independence	Survival
Courage	Influences	Traditions

Generalizations

For a theme to be effective it is essential to select generalizations or statements that focus the concept and that can be verified and/or disputed in the course of study. Generalizations of a theme are statements that serve as connectors among disciplines.

An Analogy

Think of a concept as a trip and a generalization as the path or road—an interstate highway or major route that will take you from a starting point A to a destination B. Often, there is one major path that goes from Point A to Point B. The major path will get you from A to B quickly and easily. However, if there are resources, time, and specific goals for getting from A to B, a path different from the obvious one may be chosen. The choice of path will be determined by your goals, so that goals can be accomplished along the way.

In developing curriculum for the gifted, determine what students should be able to do at the end of the unit of study. Define the *trip* with a *concept.* Define the *path* with a *generalization.*

Go back to the previous example:

TOPIC: Fairy Tales
CONCEPT: Patterns *(Trip)*
Fairy Tales: Social Studies—Geography—Map skills
Fairy Tales: English-Language Arts (ELA)—Setting—Describe the setting and patterns of travel
GENERALIZATION: Patterns are everywhere. *(Path)*

Students will explore the concept of patterns through a choice of fairly tales. They will be able to illustrate through words and graphics in what ways patterns are everywhere in their choice of fairy tale(s). Students study map skills through fairy tales. Students are asked to find patterns of travel (based on study of setting from ELA) in the fairy tales they study. They will first describe the setting in narrative form and/or with graphics. From the patterns they find, students apply map skills to develop a map for the travels of the characters in one fairy tale they select.

Concepts with Possible Generalizations

Change: Change generates change. Change can be positive or negative.

Conflict: Conflict may be natural or man made. Conflict may be intentional or unintentional.

Order: Order may have repeated patterns. Order may allow for prediction.

Patterns: Patterns have an internal order. Patterns are everywhere.

Power: Power is the ability to influence. Power is always present in some form.

Relationships: Relationships can be natural, forced, or chosen. Relationships can be simple or complex.

Structure: Structures have parts that interrelate. A structure is no stronger than its weakest component part.

Systems: Systems are composed of subsystems and parts. A system may be influenced by other systems.

Once a theme has been chosen and the generalizations determined, each discipline begins the process of organizing the content to be mastered and integrating other disciplines.

Research/Independent Study

Teachers strive to move gifted students to Tier III, which involves challenging students with independent research and projects. Tier III is the highest level of intervention for gifted students. In order to prepare students for Tier III, they must fully understand research skills. Encourage learners to expand their knowledge about the use of resources, to investigate new resources, to explore different research designs, and to complete independent studies.

When the topic of research is mentioned to students, most respond negatively. Many see research as spending hours in the library or on a computer searching through resources, taking notes, citing sources, organizing data, and writing a paper about their findings. Research is so much more than this. Research is discovering new information, preferably about a topic of interest to the student, looking at multiple perspectives, and creating a product that reflects the results in a unique way. Research does not have to be "boring," as many students would call it. Research can open a world of information, which can lead students to new discoveries, giving them a deeper understanding of the information. It can also help guide them towards a career.

The first step in research is to choose a topic. This is one of the most important parts of the process. If the topic does not arouse the student's curiosity of the subject, then most likely the experience will be a failure. The assignment may be accomplished, but with little interest and learning on the student's part. Many times, choosing the topic is the hardest part of the process. It is important to determine the student's interests using an interest inventory. This can be an informal or formal process. Many interest inventories can be found online; some are free and others can be purchased from different educational sources. Most ask questions about the student's areas of interest. Some will also address the types of products a student enjoys creating. This helps identify the student's learning style as well.

Allowing the student to use his or her prominent learning style can also be the difference between success or failure of a research project. If a specific product is required as the end result of a research project and it is out of the student's learning-style range, then little interest and, many times, less effort will be placed on the creation of that product. The more common learning styles include kinesthetic, technological, verbal, visual, and auditory. As with interest inventories, there are many formal and informal learning-styles screening measures available for educators.

In Section V, F-4, there is an example of an interest inventory, which can be used with students. F-5 can be used to help students with products in their learning-style area.

There are several different research models available for students. Most models overlap the research skills. The model discussed in this book is the Five-Step Process. It was developed by Vowery Carlile by adapting the research scaffolding from the Texas Performance Standards Project.

Five-Step Process

Once the topic has been chosen, the Five-Step Process begins. It includes Step 1, writing guiding questions; Step 2, taking notes and citing sources; Step 3, organizing information; Step 4, planning and producing a product; and Step 5, presenting the information and product. Each of these steps will be discussed in more detail.

Step 1: Once the topic has been chosen, the student is ready to write guiding questions that will be used to lead him/her in the research. Guiding questions, particularly for the gifted child, need to be written using a critical-thinking models, such as Bloom's Taxonomy. The questions should also add depth and complexity. By using these best-practice strategies in writing the guiding questions, a deeper, more complex thinking about the topic will be achieved by the student.

Step 2: It is now time to find resources that will help the student answer the guiding questions. Arrange for the school librarian to show students resources available in the library. (See example E-7 for a list of resources that can be found in most school libraries.) The Internet is also a great resource. It provides a wealth of wonderful information for students, but educators should not lose sight of the library's potential contribution. In the early years of the Internet, educators tried to teach students to understand and use it. This meant surfing the Internet to find resources for different assignments. Soon, the only resources used during research were Internet sources. A trip to the library is a great class lesson. Students must understand that there are credible and non-credible sources. One can't assume that students know how to identify reliable resources. Many sources on the Internet include inaccurate information. Students must be taught how to distinguish between credible and non-credible resources. (See the F-6 in Section V to help students with this skill.) One of the best ways to teach this skill is to find a reliable source, then let the students surf the Internet for information about their topic. Once this has been accomplished, have the students compare their sources with the reliable source. If there are discrepancies, the students need to do further research regarding their source. If credibility cannot be proven, the source needs to be discarded. Limit Internet sources so a variety of resources can be utilized for the research project. This helps to teach the students that a wide variety of resources is available for use.

Step 2 also involves teaching how to summarize, take notes, and cite sources. Students are also taught the meaning of plagiarism and how to avoid it. Each of these skills requires a lesson. To teach summarizing and notetaking, have the student write on note cards or resource pages (secondary) a few words and phrases about important points from their resource. When the time comes for the student to create their product, whether a research paper, brochure, poster, or other product, they must develop their own sentences. Not allowing students to copy information word for word or in complete sentences from a source helps to eliminate most episodes of plagiarism.

Because organization is an issue with many students, this skill has to be taught and continually reinforced. One successful method for note cards is to use a different colored card for each resource. (There is an assortment of colors in the three main sizes of note cards.) For instance, all information from a particular magazine article may be written on blue note cards. The topic of the notes is placed at the top of the note card and all information written on that card deals with that topic. Another topic covered in that resource is placed on a new blue note card and information pertaining to that topic is written on the card. (See E-8.)

There are several different ways to cite a source. Elementary and middle-school students need to be exposed to one method so less confusion occurs. The Modern Language Association (MLA) seems to be a good reference for teaching students how to cite a source. High-school students need to be informed that there are other ways to cite a source; however, only one way should be required of them for their project. Once they get to college, each professor will make known what method of citing is to be used in his or her class. There are several programs available online which teach the different methods for citing a source. Some programs require the student to input their bibliography information and choose which method to use. The bibliography is then created in the program. This is a good way to make sure the correct format is followed, yet students should be exposed to the "old fashioned" method of citing a source as well. (See E-9 for format methods of citing a source according to MLA.)

Step 3: Once the note taking has been completed and all guiding questions have been answered, formally (elementary and middle school students) or informally (high school), then the notes must be organized. This can be done through graphic organizers (elementary) or outlines (secondary).

By using an organizational folder as well as colored note cards with elementary and middle-school students, organizing notes is much easier. (See E-10 for an example of the organizational folder.) Students make their folders by gluing pockets on a folder. Each pocket is labeled with a topic from the note cards, with the first or last pocket reserved for resource information. Once the note cards are placed into the correct topic pocket, the students are ready to create their graphic organizer. Outlining is a hard skill for younger students to learn. By using a graphic organizer to introduce outlining skills, students seem to grasp the concept more easily.

Step 4: Once the organization is complete, it is time to choose a product. Whether the product is a written paper, a newscast, a magazine article, a demonstration, or a book, the information learned from the research is used to create it. With elementary students, the product is a way to show what they learned from their research and to present that information with a creative prod-uct. Middle-school students are expected to begin showing their interpretation of the information in a new way. This means that after the research is complete, students use the learned information to create and present their own perspective through the product. High-school students are expect-ed to show their understanding of the topic by creating a solution to a problem or by discovering and presenting their own viewpoint about the topic. The product allows students to share their research in a unique way. (See Section IV for a more in-depth discussion of products.)

Step 5: The last step in research is the presentation. This is very important because the students can "show-off" their work. It is a time to share what they have learned with others. The presen-tation can be compared to icing on a cake; without the icing, the cake is not "nearly as good." The research process is not "nearly as good" without the presentation.

The presentation must be well organized. In order to help students with this skill, they should use a presentation outline. (See E-11 for an example of the format that should be followed.)

Oral Presentation

One should not assume that students will know how to do an oral presentation. This is a skill that must be taught and practiced. Students are never too young to begin giving presentations. For instance, a kindergarten student may be asked to stand in front of the class and talk about the T-ball game played the afternoon before. This is a skill that requires practice. Students acquire confidence from presenting in front of peers and adults. (E-12 gives oral-presentation tips that should to be taught to students prior to their presentations.)

Students are also given an opportunity to demonstrate an understanding of the information by answering questions about their work at the end of the presentation. This is a great way to find out if they really understand what they learned from the research process.

Good presentation experience is a life skill needed to succeed in college and beyond.

A Final Note about Research: *So What?*

So What? is a term applied to the outcome of learning. Often students learn many facts about a topic that they offer to their audience. *So What?* carries their learning beyond recitation of facts. When students reflect on the meaning and outcome of their learning, they not only express their ability to learn and recite, but also accommodate their cognitive growth and ability to appraise their work. Their work leads to new learning and makes a difference for their audience.

So What? is encompassed in the Principles of Differentiation relating to the affective nature and needs of the gifted. (See below.)

- Encourage the development of self-understanding: recognizing and using one's abilities; becoming self-directed; and appreciating both the likenesses and differences between oneself and others.
- Evaluate student outcomes by using appropriate and specific criteria through self-appraisal, criterion referenced and/or standardized instruments.

So What?—not just knowledge—should be the goal for the gifted learner.

Principles of Differentiation were developed at the National/State Leadership Training Institute on the Gifted and Talented by the Curriculum Council: Joseph J. Gallagher, Sandra N. Kaplan, A. Harry Passow, Joseph S. Renzulli, Irving S. Sato, Dorothy Sisk, and Janice Wickless. 1976, Los Angeles, CA.

Bloom Questions for Elementary Students

Topic: Fairy Tales

Knowledge: List several well known fairy tales.

Comprehension: Choose one of the fairy tales and retell it to the class.

Application: Find a fairy tale that has a setting similar to somewhere that you have visited. Tell about it.

Analysis: Choose two fairy tales and compare them. Use a Venn diagram to show your work.

Synthesis: Change places with the two main characters in each fairy tale. Predict how the story might be different.

Evaluation: Of the two stories you chose, which is your favorite and why?

Bloom Questions for Secondary Students

Topic: The Civil War

Knowledge: When and where did the turning point occur in the Civil War?

Comprehension: Explain the reasons for the Civil War.

Application: Construct a diagram which shows the losses of life that occurred on each side during the Civil War.

Analysis: Distinguish the differences between the North and South that relate to the economy of the country.

Synthesis: Predict what might have happened had the South won instead of the North. How might this have impacted civil rights today?

Evaluation: Had you lived during this tragic time in America's history, which side would you have represented and why?

Bloom Question Stems and Activities

Application: Question Stems

- Do you know another instance where…?
- What factors would you change if…?
- Would this information be useful if you had a…?
- What question would you ask of…?
- Can you apply the method used to some experiment of your own…?
- Could this have happened in…?
- Can you group characteristics such as…?

Application: Activities

- Construct a model to demonstrate how it will work.
- Make a scrapbook about the areas of study.
- Paint a mural using the same materials.
- Design a market strategy for your product using a known strategy as a model.
- Dress a doll in national costume.
- Take a collection of photographs to demonstrate a particular point.
- Make up a puzzle game pursuing the ideas from the study.
- Write a textbook about…for others.

Analysis: Question Stems

- How would you compare your…with that presented in…?
- How would you explain what must have happened when…?
- How would you distinguish between…and…?
- If…had happened, what might the ending have been?
- How was…similar to…?
- What was the underlying theme of…?
- What are the differences between…and…?
- What do you see as other possible outcomes?

Bloom Question Stems and Activities, continued

Analysis: Activities

- Make a family tree showing relationships.
- Prepare a report about the area of study.
- Design a questionnaire to gather information.
- Make a flow chart to show the critical stages of….
- Create a Power Point presentation to explain the differences between…and….
- Use graffiti writing to explain the underlying meaning of….
- Write a biography about….
- Write a commercial to sell a new product.

Synthesis: Question Stems

- How can…be used to create a new…?
- What would happen if…?
- Develop a proposal to…?
- What might be a new and unusual use for…?
- What might be a possible solution to…?
- How would you compose a song using…'s music style?
- How would you design a…to do…?
- What might have happened had the end result been different?

Synthesis: Activities

- Create a new product. Give it a name and plan a marketing campaign.
- Design a new energy-efficient home.
- Compose a rhyme or put new words to a known melody.
- Invent a machine to do a specific task.
- Choose a popular story and rewrite it with a new twist to the plot.
- Develop a plan as a possible solution to a community problem.
- Suppose you could change one thing on…. Illustrate the change.
- Design the costumes for a play written by you.

Bloom Question Stems and Activities, continued

Evaluation: Question Stems

- Is there a better solution to…?
- What is the value of…?
- How would you defend your position about…?
- How would you have handled…? Explain your answer.
- Can you recommend a specific book, T.V. show, or movie to a friend? Explain why.
- What changes would you make to…? Why?
- Do you think…is good or bad? Why?
- How would you feel if…happened to you? Explain.

Evaluation: Activities

- Prepare a list of criteria to judge a T.V. show.
- Make a booklet about five rules you see as important. Convince others.
- Write a letter to…stating the need for changes to….
- Conduct a debate about an issue of special interest.
- Justify your actions.
- Select a favorite movie and write a movie review about it.
- Discuss an issue you feel strongly about with a friend.
- Create a new set of rules for the class and justify each.

Critical Thinking

THE PROBLEM

Your mentor, the mayor of your city, leaves a message for you to meet her at the city swimming pool on the south side of town during your lunch period. She has talked with your principal to get permission for you to stay with her for the remainder of the school day. She says that you need to bring old clothing and shoes. She wants you to study the situation and make a recommendation and presentation for the city council.

Your city has two swimming pools: an old one in the southern part of town called Park Cities (Park) and a new one in the north with water slides and sports areas called The Slides of Glenview (Slides). Both are connected to a park area.

You remember that there have been issues with Park for the past year. These issues stem from its location and its age. The pool is forty years old and is situated next to an old fertilizer plant. The pool was shut down at the end of the swimming season last year because of fears of leakage from the fertilizer storage tanks and the old, often repaired cracks in the pool. About six months ago the city council decided to close Park permanently.

Many of the town's citizens disagreed with the council's decision. For the past six months citizens representing both sides of the issue have appeared before the council to express their opinions. Today the mayor and council are meeting with local citizens; engineers; representatives from the EPA (Environmental Protection Agency); a scientist who specializes in groundwater contamination; and the county representative from Parks and Wildlife; who could provide funding for rehabilitation of the pool. The purpose of the meeting is to collect data in order to make a decision about the future of the pool.

The citizens are anxious for the council to either rescind or maintain its decision because swimming season opens in four weeks.

Complete your own Reasoning Model. Describe your decision-making process and prepare a presentation for the next city council meeting.

REASONING MODEL* FOR
PROBLEM-BASED LEARNING

*Form adapted from R. Paul, 1992

Aim

to determine the future of the Park pool

Viewpoints

citizens, local government, EPA, scientist, Parks & Wildlife representatives, engineers

Facts

leakage from fertilizer storage tanks, age of pool, cracks in pool

Opinion Statement

The pool needs to be open for the citizens of the south side of the city.

ISSUE / PROBLEM

Contamination of water in the swimming pool

Suppositions

All parties want a decision made. Citizens living in the south side of the city want their pool open. The city government wants facts about contamination.

Concept and Generalization

Relationships: Relationships can be positive or negative.

Consequences

If the area must be cleaned up before opening, cost must be considered.
If the pool remains closed, all citizens must use the Slides.

REASONING MODEL FOR PROBLEM-BASED LEARNING

CONCEPT/THEME: STRUCTURE
GENERALIZATION: Structures have parts that interrelate.

This unit provides a curriculum example that addresses the concept (trip) and generalization (path) and illustrates how topics and facts define the learning outcome.

<u>Topics</u> demonstrated and integrated into the unit:

Measurement (Math)   Safety (Health & Physical Education)

Technology (Tech. Applications)   Writing (English-Language Arts)

<u>Facts</u> to support students' knowledge and skills to address the theory, concept, and products of the unit.

Metric or U.S. measurement   Measuring length, area and perimeter

Drawing to scale (ratio)   Area to be used

Needs of playground users   Types of playground equipment

Technical writing   Persuasive writing

LEARNING SCENARIO:

A new middle school is being constructed. The students of the school see the architects' designs and determine that there will be enough space around the new building for parking without using an area in back of the building that contains several shade trees. Their idea is to create a space for all the students to have for daily exercise, organized sports, and pick-up games.

CURRICULUM CONNECTION

The students ask to go ahead with their plans to petition the administration and local board of education for their desired use of the space. Teachers and students together determine that the solution to their problem will include a scale model of a playground using the U.S. Customary Measurement System or the Metric System. The problem includes issues of health and safety. Through an exploration of safety issues, students determine the placement of equipment such as tetherball, a volleyball court, and a croquet field.

The purpose of the scale model is to exemplify learning for an authentic audience and to accommodate rigor in learning as the students analyze, synthesize, and evaluate their knowledge, comprehension, and application.

REASONING MODEL, continued

Students determine standards and skills required and related to measurement (length, area, and perimeter), drawing to scale, types of equipment, requirements of users, safety facts, physical area to be used, how to graph and communicate through technology, and how to write both technically and persuasively. These facts form the foundation of the study.

Pre-assessment

PURPOSE: To determine if students recognize the scope of the project: math, physical education, health, technology, persuasive writing, and technical writing.

A timeline will show that students understand the math, physical education, health, technology, and writing and other communication skills necessary to complete the project. If students don't understand timelines, create one for the classroom that shows the steps and times you have set as your expectations for completing each sector of the curriculum.

HINT FOR TIMELINES: Google "timelines" if you think students need examples.

This work should be done individually so that you know how to proceed. For example, if students have the math skills, understand safety issues and the scope of equipment, and are skilled in persuasive writing, but lack skills of technical writing and technology, the latter are the only areas that must be addressed as they work on their plan.

WHAT IF?
What if only some of your students complete pre-assessment to your satisfaction? How will you manage a classroom that has some students working on one sector and others working in another? (See Classroom Management in Section III for examples.)

Activities

Students connect their health, physical education, math, technology facts, and writing skills to apply knowledge of the interrelationship among equipment, physical placement of the equipment, health and safety issues that influence their choices, technology that facilitates their final product development, and writing skills that make possible communication about their plans. Students apply the knowledge gained from learning facts from each of the content areas.

EXAMPLE: What kinds of information will you need to complete the project? Make a list. From the list, create a problem for each item that shows you know the skills for that item. For instance, you will need to measure the area to know how much space is available for the athletic area.

PRACTICE PROBLEM: Measure the area of your classroom.

Students are working on the analysis (analyzing), synthesis, and evaluation (judging and creating) levels of Bloom's Taxonomy. Provide the rubric for students to assess their preparation and learning in this sector. The rubric is found at the end of this section.

Students will determine placement of athletic equipment, giving attention to safety, size, and needs of the ages who will participate in activities. They will describe their plans in technical writing terms.

Students will begin to plan their presentation, including technology and persuasive writing.

Students begin work on the solution to their problem; work will include a scale model of the outdoor area using the U.S. Customary Measurement System or the Metric System.

Through an exploration of safety issues, students determine the placement of ment such as tetherball, a volleyball court, and a croquet field.

The purpose of the scale model is to exemplify learning for an authentic audience and to accommodate rigor in learning as the students analyze, synthesize, and evaluate their knowledge, comprehension, and application.

As students work on their problem, they verify their learning through analysis and synthesis of the topics of measurement, safety, technology, and ELA with the facts from content areas, validating or invalidating knowledge and its application embedded in students' complex analysis and synthesis of the content. Students determine health and safety components that influence their equipment choices and placements on the outdoor area. Activities are designed to teach students how to critically and creatively solve problems—in this case, how to determine their course of action in order to produce the scale model and present it to the school board and administration.

Problem-based Learning Rubrics to Evaluate Problem Scenario & Activities

Students' Rubric

	The Goal	Almost	Getting There	BLAH!
THEME	Allows for students to see relevance that leads to understanding.	Allows for relevance, but is too broad or too narrow to include all learning.	Is too broad or too narrow so that learning is unfocused.	Is really a topic. Does not provide the big picture for the students.
GENERALIZATION	Focuses students on the theme.	Is too broad to focus students' learning or too narrow to focus students on theme.	Is a generalization, but does not match the theme.	Is a statement, not a generalization.
TOPIC	Is relevant for the students.	Is relevant, but too focused on school topics.	Is relevant for school topics only.	Is not relevant to age and stage of students.
STATE STANDARDS	Relevant to theme, generalization, and topic. Broad enough to integrate across disciplines.	Either relevant to theme, generalization, and topic or broad enough to integrate across disciplines, but not both.	Is neither relevant to theme, generalization, and topic nor broad enough to integrate across disciplines.	Includes standards from one discipline only.

Curriculum Rubric

	The Goal	Almost	Getting There	BLAH!
CONTENT	Allows for rigor in activities that are integrated so that students see relevance leading to their understanding.	Includes integration but may not allow for relevance or include rigorous activities.	Is too broad or too narrow so that learning is unfocused.	Is in one content area only.
INSTRUCTIONAL ACTIVITIES	Activities are integrated, relevant to students, allow for testing of theory, related to theme and principle or generalization, are rigorous, and allow for understanding.	Activities are integrated, but lack 1 of the following: relevance to students, testing of theory, related to theme and generalization, or rigorous.	Activities are integrated, but lack more than 1 of the following: relevance to students, testing of theory, related to theme and generalization, or rigorous.	Activities are not integrated.

Curriculum Rubric, continued

	The Goal	Almost	Getting There	BLAH!
DEFENSE	Defense relates to choices and allows the reader to see the relation of the choice to the theory, theme, generalization, topic, and standards.	Defense relates to choices but does not allow the reader to see the relation of the choice to one of the following: theory, theme, generalization, topic, and standards.	Defense relates to choices but does not allow the reader to see the relation of the choice to more than one of the following: theory, theme, principle or generalization, topic, and standards.	Defense is unrelated to the task or there is no defense.
THEME	Focuses students on the theme.	Allows for relevance, but is too broad or too narrow to include all learning.	Is too broad or too narrow so that learning is unfocused.	Is really a topic. Does not provide the big picture for the students.
PRINCIPLE/ GENERALIZATION	Allows for students to see relevance that leads to understanding.	Is too broad to focus students' learning or too narrow to focus students on theme.	Is a principle or generalization, but does not match the theme.	Is a statement, not a generalization.
TOPIC	Is relevant for the students.	Is relevant, but too focused on school topics.	Is relevant for school topics only.	Is not relevant to age and stage of students.
CONTENT/ STATE STANDARDS	Relevant to theme, generalization and topic. Broad enough to integrate across disciplines.	Either relevant to theme, generalization and topic or broad enough to integrate across disciplines, but not both.	Is neither relevant to theme, generalization and topic nor broad enough to integrate across disciplines.	Includes standards from one discipline only.
INSTRUCTIONAL STRATEGIES	Activities are integrated, relevant to students, allow for testing of theory, related to theme and principle or generalization, are rigorous, and allow for understanding.	Activities are integrated, but lack one of the following: relevant to students, allow for testing of theory, relate to theme and generalization, rigor, or allow for understanding.	Activities are integrated, but lack more than one of the following: relevant to students, allow for testing of theory, relate to theme and generalization, rigor, or allow for EUREKA!	Activities are not integrated.

ENGLISH / LANGUAGE ARTS / READING

ACTIVITY:

Write a two-minute speech to persuade your classmates to participate in one of the following activities:

tetherball	baseball	basketball	flag football
running	jogging	walking	monkey bars
volleyball	croquet	lifting weights	

Present your speech to the class using a combination of writing, speaking, and technology.

MATH

Patterns, relationships, and algebraic thinking

Measurement

Underlying processes and mathematical tools

ACTIVITY:

Measure the length and width of the flat surface of your desk, the teacher's desk, and one other surface in the classroom, first in feet and inches and then using metric measurement.

For each of the three surfaces estimate the perimeter and area, first using U.S. Customary Measurement and then using the Metric System.

	YOUR DESK feet/inches	YOUR DESK metric	TEACHER'S DESK feet/inches	TEACHER'S DESK metric	OTHER SURFACE feet/inches	OTHER SURFACE metric
Estimated Perimeter						
Estimated Area						
Comparison to Your Height: feet/inches and metric measure						

PROBLEM: Determine the relationship, if any, among the perimeters and areas of the three surfaces and your height. Show your findings in a circle or bar graph.

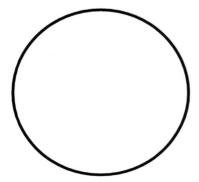

CULMINATING ACTIVITY

CONCEPT/THEME: STRUCTURE
GENERALIZATION: Parts of structures support and are supported by other
parts.

ACTIVITY:
Students will determine the placement of athletic equipment giving attention to safety, size, and the needs and ages of the children who will participate in activities. Students describe their plans in technical writing terms.

Students will begin to plan their presentation, including technology and persuasive writing.

TECHNOLOGY

ACTIVITY:

Create a five-slide PowerPoint presentation that includes information from at least two Internet sources on the topic of safety regarding one of the following activities:

tetherball	**baseball**	**basketball**	**flag football**
running	**jogging**	**walking**	**monkey bars**
volleyball	**croquet**	**lifting weights**	

OR

Present your information to the class using one or more of the following:

- graphics
- video
- audio
- poster with images from the Internet

HINTS FOR TECHNICAL WRITING:

- Include definitions of terms.
- Use shorter paragraphs.
- Use active verbs.
- Use shorter sentences.
- Include headings, lists, and graphics.

CREATIVE PROBLEM SOLVING

FACTS:

- Young adolescents are seen walking the streets after 11:00 p.m.
- Teens are getting into trouble with the law; vandalism, stealing, and gang-related activities are becoming more prevalent.

PROBLEM: Students who are not involved in school-related activities are getting into trouble.

IDEAS:

- Impose curfew
- Fine parents
- More activities to keep teens busy
- Character-building activities

SOLUTION: Create a chart to evaluate the ideas.

Place a plus sign (+) under an idea for a positive evaluation and a minus sign (–) for a negative evaluation. Count the +'s and the –'s. Each + gets 3 points and each – gets 1 point. No points are allotted if left blank.

CRITERIA	Curfew	Fine Parents	More Activities	Character-Building Activities
Cost	+	+	–	–
Within the law	+	+	+	+
Motivates teens to stay out of trouble	–	+	+	+
TALLY	2 +, 1 –	3 +, 0 –	2 +, 1 –	2 +, 1 –

IDEA	NO. POSITIVE x 3	NO. NEGATIVE x -1	TOTAL POINTS
Curfew	2 x 3 = 6	1 x -1 = -1	6 – 1 = 5
Parents fined	3 x 3 = 9	0 x -1 = 0	9 – 0 = 9
More activities	2 x 3 = 6	1 x -1 = -1	6 - 1 = 5
Character-building activities	2 x 3 = 6	1 x -1 = -1	6 - 1 = 5

The idea with the most points is the possible solution to the problem.

Solution: Parents should be fined if their kids are in trouble with the law for vandalism, stealing, or gang-related activities more than once.

CREATIVE PROBLEM SOLVING, continued

ACCEPTANCE FINDING:

What are the steps needed to solve the problem?

- Write a city ordinance which addresses the solution.
- Notify the community through written communication and a city-wide meeting of the new ordinance and the consequences for parents if teens disobey the ordinance.
- Follow the city ordinance consistently.
- Possibly use the money obtained from the fines to help create a Student Activity Center.

Culminating Activity:

Students could research the following topics that might provide further solutions to the problem and create a plan of implementation.

- Inexpensive activities that would provide entertainment for teens
- Community-service projects that would provide work for those teens
- Solutions that other communities of the same size have used

SCAMPER

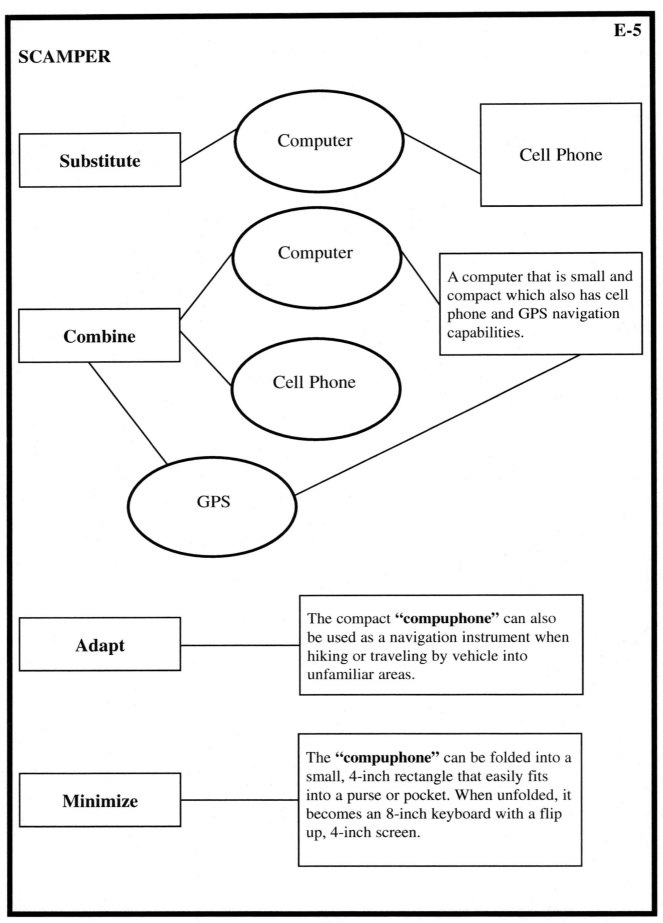

Substitute — Computer — Cell Phone

Combine — Computer, Cell Phone, GPS — A computer that is small and compact which also has cell phone and GPS navigation capabilities.

Adapt — The compact **"compuphone"** can also be used as a navigation instrument when hiking or traveling by vehicle into unfamiliar areas.

Minimize — The **"compuphone"** can be folded into a small, 4-inch rectangle that easily fits into a purse or pocket. When unfolded, it becomes an 8-inch keyboard with a flip up, 4-inch screen.

SCAMPER, continued

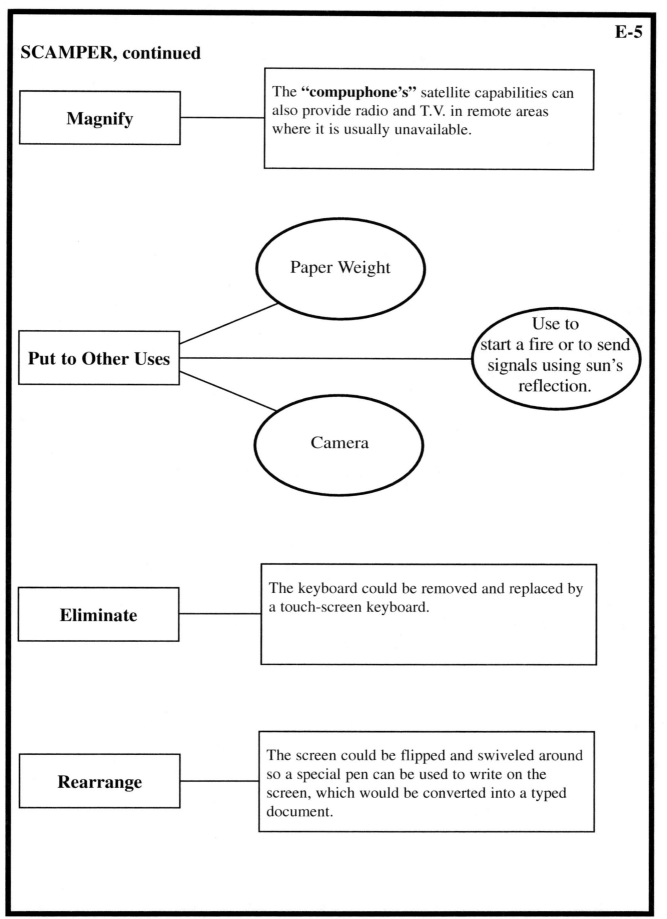

Magnify

The **"compuphone's"** satellite capabilities can also provide radio and T.V. in remote areas where it is usually unavailable.

Paper Weight

Put to Other Uses

Use to start a fire or to send signals using sun's reflection.

Camera

Eliminate

The keyboard could be removed and replaced by a touch-screen keyboard.

Rearrange

The screen could be flipped and swiveled around so a special pen can be used to write on the screen, which would be converted into a typed document.

DEPTH AND COMPLEXITY

DETAILS

Elaborate on **recycling**.

EXAMPLE: *reduce, reuse, recycle, glass, plastic, paper, metals*

Questions that elicit details:
- Which details are more important than others?
- Who are important people?
- What are important places and events?

LANGUAGE OF THE DISCIPLINE

In what way is **recycling** best communicated?

EXAMPLE: *change, environment, conserve*

ACTIVITY
The following activity addresses the language of a journalist:

Write an article as a journalist would for your local or school newspaper. Discuss effects upon the environment, conservation issues, and changes that can occur with recycling.

PATTERNS

Identify the political, social, and economic patterns associated with **recycling.**

ACTIVITY
The following discussion activity elicits observations of patterns:

When the economy is good, recycling is supported by politicians and society.

RULES

What are the reasons, motives, or events that underlie **recycling?**

Create a list that draws out the underlying rules of recycling:

- importance of having a clean earth

DEPTH AND COMPLEXITY, continued

TRENDS

What ongoing influences caused/affected **recycling?**

Students could answer the generalization "Influences can be positive or negative" when looking for trends. Students can look for positive and negative influences in the economy, advertising, or organizations.

UNANSWERED QUESTIONS

What ideas remain unclear or incomplete about **recycling?**

The following question could spur students' thinking about unanswered questions:

How much money is spent on recycling each year and how does it impact the economy and natural resources?

ETHICS

What ethical issues surround **recycling?**

Students could explore negative influences to spark this discussion and research. (See "Trends.")

Is recycling really helping to conserve natural resources? Take into consideration the energy used to recycle.

BIG IDEA

What general statement summarizes **recycling?**

The following statement is an example of the big idea:

Conserve natural resources and keep the earth clean by recycling.

The above statement is encumbered in the concept of Influences. (See Concept-based Learning.)

DEPTH AND COMPLEXITY, continued

OVER TIME

How is **recycling** relating to the past, present, and future?

Initiate the discussion with the following:

One hundred fifty years ago there was no need for recycling because there were no aluminum cans, no cardboard, and few glass bottles. Recycling is important to the *present* because by recycling *now,* natural resources can be protected, which will impact our *future*. What types of products will be required to be recycled in the future?

MULTIPLE PERSPECTIVES

How do different people see **recycling?**

Each of the following sees recycling in a different light:

- Politicians: If the economy is good, recycling can be an issue for elections, but if it is poor, recycling is not important.
- Environmentalists: Even people who are protective of the environment will not support recycling if it means putting a recycling factory somewhere that might not be pleasing to the eye or that would endanger or disturb animals or their habitats.
- Others factors to consider when thinking about points of view towards recycling might include impact on particular communities, industry, rural areas, or different age groups.

ACROSS THE DISCIPLINES

Compare the effects of **recycling** on industry and the environment.

Compare and contrast the following:

- Industry: Recycling creates jobs which stimulates the economy.
- Environment: Recycling helps to keep the environment clean and conserves natural resources.

Author's Note: I make an envelope book for each child. I use a medium envelope for the cover and back of the book, adding 12 pages with one of the depth and complexity elements on each page. We discuss each element. The students write examples on the page and then draw a picture that will help them remember the element. After completing the study, students look through magazines, cut out pictures that could be used with the elements, label them and place them in the envelopes, which serve as the front and back covers of the book.

DEPTH AND COMPLEXITY

Secondary Lesson: *COURAGE*

UNANSWERED QUESTIONS

Initiate unanswered questions with a chart: What do we *know* about courage? What do we *want* to know about courage? What did you *learn* about courage? This provides a base of knowledge, expands the base for all the students in the group, and provides opportunity for unanswered questions that lead to independent studies.

K-W-L Chart

K What do you **know** about courage?	**W** What do you **want** to know about courage?	**L** What did you **learn** about courage?

LANGUAGE OF THE DISCIPLINE

Discuss courage and generate a list of names of courageous people (fictional or actual). What terms are used to describe courage or courageous acts? Use the following questions to guide thinking:

- Who is the most courageous person you know or have seen or read about (either fictional or actual)?
- What words are used/would you use to describe the person's courage or courageous act(s)?

DEPTH AND COMPLEXITY

Secondary Lesson: *COURAGE,* continued

DETAILS

What are the attributes of courage? How do you know someone is courageous? Elaborate on the descriptions found during the Language of the Discipline activities.

The following activity elicits details:

Describe through drawings or narrative the attributes of courage. Use the information you found during the Language of the Discipline activities.

PATTERNS

When do people find courage? What are the origins of heroes?

Patterns may be uncovered while thinking about and answering these questions:

- In what ways are courage or courageous acts shaped by social, political, and economic influences?
- Are there different patterns associated with courage that are dependent upon one of the influences above? Defend your answer.

TRENDS, RELATIONSHIPS OVER TIME, AND ACROSS DISCIPLINES

To incorporate the element of depth and the two elements of complexity ask students to answer this question: Are courageous acts and/or the heroes who display them always the same?

Then ask them to talk with their parents and grandparents to determine the kinds of heroes that other generations have had and the acts they considered courageous. Heroes could be divided into **Traditional Heroes,** such as Superman, Batman, or any of the comic-book superheros, and **Inspirational Heroes,** such as people in the community and people in the military. In both cases, students should be instructed to try to identify why these people are heroes and why their acts are viewed as courageous.

RULES

Why do heroes behave as they do? Are there rules for heroes or the courage they display?

To find more about the rules and to answer these questions, students complete this activity:

Compare and contrast the courage displayed by heroes from your grandparents' generation, heroes from your parents' generation, and those you have identified.

DEPTH AND COMPLEXITY, continued

Secondary Lesson: *COURAGE,* continued

ETHICS AND BIG IDEA

What ethics are associated with courage?

Students relate their query through the big idea, or concept, of *courage*. What general statement summarizes courage?

Courage may be viewed as positive or negative.

- When is a heroic act viewed as a positive? Give examples.
- Are there times that a heroic act could be viewed negatively? Give examples.

Other generalizations that could be used for a different discussion of ethics:

- The definition of *courage* is dependent on the person/people involved in the situation.
- Courageous acts create heroes.

DIFFERENT PERSPECTIVES/POINTS OF VIEW

Does courage exist in the animal kingdom? Why or why not? Write a short story that exemplifies your perspective. A piece of literature such as *The Lion and the Mouse* may provide a foundation for this examination.

INTERDISCIPLINARY RELATIONSHIPS

Connect art or music to the hero or courageous acts.

For example, students may consider one of the following:

- In what musical ways are courageous acts presented? Provide musical examples.
- What famous artists painted ordinary heroes? Explain.

RESOURCES

PRIMARY RESOURCES

Primary sources are usually unpublished and provide firsthand knowledge about the topic. For instance, explorers kept journals about their experiences, places they visited, and people they met along their journeys. Because these journals are based upon firsthand experiences, they would be considered primary sources.

interview	manuscripts
photographs	surveys
maps	observations
artifacts	audio and video recordings
oral histories	posters
postcards	experiments

SECONDARY RESOURCES

A secondary source involves information that is written by someone. A secondary resource can also be an interpretation of a primary source, such as a textbook, a newspaper article, or an encyclopedia, to list a few.

Books:

fiction	almanacs
nonfiction	dictionary
biography	encyclopedia

Electronic Sources:

database	compact discs	audio cassettes
Internet	records	computer program
movies	filmstrips	videotape

Newspapers

Note Cards

TOOLS
hammer
saw
drill

JOBS
mechanic
carpenter
fisherman

Bibliography

A bibliography is an alphabetical list of all the resources used during research. It is a way to give credit to the source used by the author. There are many different ways to cite sources. The following are examples of how to cite sources according to the MLA (Modern Language Association). NOTE: Every line after the first line of the citing is indented.

BOOK BY ONE AUTHOR:

Author's last name, first name. *Title of book.* City where published: Publisher's name, Year of publication.

EXAMPLE:

Fort, Sandy. *Where Do the Birds Go in the Winter?* New York, NY: Render Publishing Company, 2007.

BOOK BY TWO OR MORE AUTHORS: (The first author named will go first.)

First author's last name, first name and second author's first and last names. City where published: Publisher's name, Year of publication.

EXAMPLE:

Barber, Shelley and Vince McGuire. *North American Birds.* London: New World Press, 2008.

INTERNET SOURCE:

Author, if available, listed the same as a book. If no author is listed, "Title of Article" Date visited and the URL address.

EXAMPLE:

"Birds of the South" November 6, 2008. http://www.birds/south.com

ENCYCLOPEDIAS AND OTHER RESOURCE BOOKS:

Author's last name, first name. "Title of article." *Title of Reference Book.* Year of the edition used.

EXAMPLE:

Rugger, Steve. "Birds." *The Encyclopedia of Birds.* 2008.

MAGAZINES AND JOURNALS:

Author's last name, first name. "Title of Article." *Magazine Name.* Date on magazine.

EXAMPLE:

Santon, Chris. "Birds of a Feather." *Bird World.* November 2, 2007.

PERSONAL INTERVIEW: Last name, first name. Personal interview. Date interviewed.

Organizational Folder

Resources

Topic

Topic

Topic

Topic

Topic

Presentation Outline

Organize your presentation using the following outline. No matter what product you choose, you will have to present your information orally to the class. Use notes to help you present your research and your product.

I. Introduction

    A. Include the topic with a catchy statement.

    B. Grab the audience's attention.

II. Body

    A. This will be the major part of the presentation of your product.

    B. Include important information.

    C. Know your information so that you refer to your notes as little as possible.

    D. Show any visuals you have included.

III. Conclusion

    A. Summarize your presentation in one or two sentences.

    B. Do not include any new material.

    C. Ask for questions.

    D. Answer the questions to the best of your ability.

Oral Presentation Tips

1. Know your topic and material well.

2. Be organized. Have your materials and information ready to use in your presentation.
   - Practice your presentation.
   - Do not read your presentation.
   - Give your presentation to anyone who will listen. Practice with your parents, your siblings, even your pets. The more often you give the presentation, the better and more comfortable you will become.

4. Make good eye contact with your audience.

5. Stand up straight, move a little, and don't stand in a frozen stance.

6. Use an oral presentation format:
   - Introduce your topic.
   - Explain each point you are trying to make.
   - Summarize your presentation with one or two sentences.
   - Ask if there are any questions.

7. Never turn your back on the audience.

8. Make sure your audience can hear and understand you.
   - Speak loudly enough so everyone can hear you.
   - Speak slowly and clearly so everyone can understand you.

Section II

Research-based Strategies

- Identifying Similarities & Differences
- Nonlinguistic Representations
- Depth and Complexity
- Cooperative Learning
- Generating & Testing Hypotheses

Research-based Strategies

As society changes, so does the need for different educational strategies. Research conducted on education in 1966 by James Coleman painted a bleak picture. The report, *Equality of Educational Opportunity,* stated that it doesn't matter what the teacher does in the classroom—that students are influenced by outside forces that cannot be changed or controlled. This caused teachers to pose the question "What does it matter how committed I am to educating students if it won't make a difference." Fortunately, current research has proved the Coleman Report wrong. Researchers such as Jere Brophy and Thomas Good (1986) refuted those old beliefs. William Sanders and his colleagues (1994, 1997) also found that the individual classroom teacher has more of an impact on student achievement than previously realized. Their research found that the most important factor affecting student learning is the teacher and after that, the strategies used in teaching the student.

Research has identified the best instructional strategies used to educate students. These have become known as researched-based strategies. Not only do these strategies improve struggling students' achievement, they also raise the test scores of average students and allow gifted students to reach their potential. Research-based strategies for G/T students are used in Tier II and Tier III to address gifted students' needs by giving them the opportunities to acquire a deeper understanding of new knowledge.

There are nine different instructional strategies that Robert J. Marzano and his associates (2001) have identified. These strategies can be used as interventions for gifted education services. They include identifying similarities and differences; summarizing and notetaking; reinforcing effort and providing recognition; homework and practice; nonlinguistic representations; cooperative learning; setting objectives and providing feedback; generating and testing hypotheses; and questions, cues, and advanced organizers that arouse interest in the topic about to be studied. This section of *Response To Intervention (RTI) for the Gifted* presents four of the nine intervention strategies. These include identifying similarities and differences, nonlinguistic representations, cooperative learning, and generating and testing hypotheses.

Identifying Similarities & Differences

Identifying similarities and differences is an intervention strategy that helps learners to see patterns and make connections. It is a fundamental cognitive process. There are various activities that can be used to teach this skill. These include Venn diagrams, T-charts, sentence frames, and card sorts. By allowing students to compare things with commonalities and contrast things that have differences, students begin to make connections at a higher level. Examples are the use of metaphors and analogies. This helps the brain process new information, recall it, and learn by overlaying a known pattern onto an unknown one to find similarities and differences. These strategies encourage students to ask questions such as "What do I already know that will help me learn this new idea?" Students are guided into a greater understanding of new learning, helping them make connections and see relationships by bringing in their own experiences and knowledge. (Gentner & Markman, 1994; Medin, Goldstone, & Markman, 1995). Further discussion of these activities is needed.

Venn Diagram

A Venn diagram uses two or more circles or ovals to compare attributes and characteristics of things such as people, places, events, or ideas. One topic is placed in "A" and another in "B." Unique characteristics for "A" are listed in "A." The same for is done for "B." "C" holds the similarities of "A" and "B." See example E-13 for a completed Venn diagram. A blank Venn diagram can be found in Section V, F-7.

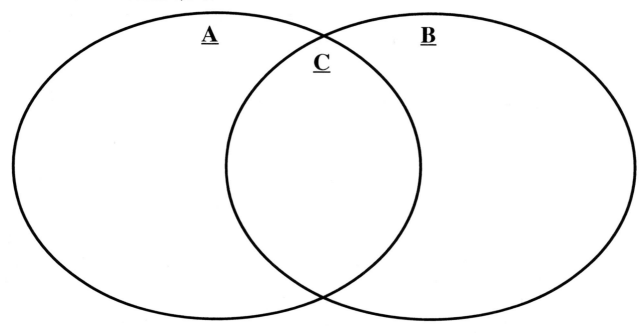

T-Chart

A T-chart is another way to make comparisons. People, places, ideas or things to be compared are placed on the top line of the T-chart. Beneath it write the two types of information to be compared. See E-14 for a completed T-chart. A blank T-chart can be found in Section V, F-8.

TOPICS TO BE COMPARED

SIMILARITIES	DIFFERENCES

Sentence Frames

Sentence frames are a way to help learners connect their background to new knowledge. When creating a sentence frame, the first sentence should start with the concept or theme.

> EXAMPLE: "What do you know about (topic)?

The second sentence should begin to draw in their experiences.

> EXAMPLE: "I know that (topic) could be used in _____ because I learned _____.

Students can also make comparisons to concrete objects.

> EXAMPLE: A _____ is like a _____ because _____.

A horse is like a car because it gets you places.

See E-15 for a completed sentence frame. A blank sentence frame can be found in Section V, F-9.

Card Sort

A strategy used to encourage students to categorize and force relationships is card sorting. This technique helps students create categories of people, places, ideas, or things. This can be taken to a higher level by forcing new categories from the obvious.

How to create a card-sort game:

- Place the name of an item to be categorized on each card. (The number of cards will be decided by the number of items to be categorized.)
- Randomize cards.
- Divide students into groups of two or three.
- Make sure students understand the directions for the game.
- Pass out the cards and have students categorize them. Do not give them the specific categories.
- Have students name the categories when finished.
- For a structured sort, give them specific category names or tell them how many categories they must create.
- To force higher-level thinking, after the students have finished a two-category sort, have them create a third category with the cards.

See examples of Card Sort Games in E-16. A blank set of cards is in Section V, F-10.

Nonlinguistic Representations

Most instruction that takes place in the classroom is through the linguistic mode; however, students can acquire and retain new information through nonlinguistic activities. Teachers using nonlinguistic activities allow students to use methods such as maps, idea webs, dramatizations, kinesthetic or whole-body modes, role play, demonstrations, models, illustrations, or pictographs, to name a few. Computer simulations also encourage learning experiences through manipulation of learning which leads to a visual result. The use of nonlinguistic representations is an intervention that often leads to new questions and discussions, which in turn encourages deeper thinking and a better understanding of the information.

Graphic Organizers

There are many different types of graphic organizers: Venn diagram, T-chart, time-sequence patterns, graphs, and charts. A graphic organizer is a way to organize information. Below is an example of a graphic organizer to be used for character analysis in a story.

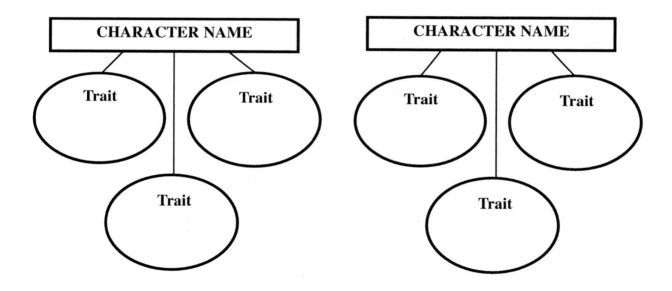

Graphic organizers can be used for cause/effect, concept attainment, generalization/principle patterns, or just to give students a mental picture of the knowledge being learned. See the blank graphic organizers in Section V, F-11.

Kinesthetic

Kinesthetic activities engage students in physical movement. These activities help students create a mental image of the concept being taught, which helps them to understand and retain the information. An example of this can be found in a lesson on verbs. A student must use physical movement to show the verb "jump."

Another way to use kinesthetic activities is by creating a people graph. Students are given specific questions about the topic. These questions can be a pre- or post-assessment. Once students have answered the questions, they are asked to line up according to their answers, forming a human graph.

Role Play

Another way to help students understand new information is through role play. Students will be asked to assume the role of characters, ideas, things, or a concept. By allowing students to "act out" the idea, they tend to gain a better understanding of the concept and better retain the knowledge. This gives the student a foundation for deeper thinking about the information.

Demonstrations, Models, Illustrations, Pictographs

According to research, students learn and retain information best by being actively involved in the learning process. When a student is asked to demonstrate or model an idea or concept, that student gains a greater understanding of the information. Students are sometimes asked to illustrate their idea or perception of the concept. This helps them create a mental image of the information in their head.

Pictographs are another form of illustrating the new learning. When the teacher has completed the lesson, students are asked to graffiti draw what they have learned about the lesson. Graffiti drawing is drawing a picture that helps them relate what they have learned about the concept. Future viewing of the picture or pictograph will help the student to remember the new information. This can be taken to a higher level by having the gifted students create new ideas about the concept through a pictograph.

Cooperative Learning

Cooperative learning uses strategies that involve interaction among students during the learning process. This can involve pairs of students, small groups, or large groups. It is a way to encourage team building among students, to boost self-esteem, and to promote social skills. Because many gifted students have problems fitting into a social setting, cooperative learning is a great opportunity to let them be "one of the team." It encourages students to work together for educational outcomes.

When creating cooperative groups consider the goal for each group's work. For example, is your goal for students to learn to work together? If so, students could be placed in groups made up of varying abilities. Is your goal is for student growth through content development? If so, students should be grouped according to ability. Gifted students progress faster and learn in more complex ways when working together.

There are many activities that promote cooperative learning. Some of these include Think-Pair Share, Fact-or-Fiction, Toss-A-Question, Stand and Share, and Find Someone Who….

Think-Pair Share

Think-Pair Share is an activity that promotes thinking skills. It was created by a professor, Frank Lyman, and his associates at the University of Maryland Howard County Southern Teacher Education Center. This activity begins with the teacher stating a problem. Students are allowed to think alone about the problem for a specific amount of time. Once time has been called, students pair up and discuss the question with their teammate. Students are asked to share their ideas with the whole class. Below are examples for Think-Pair Share.

Elementary

List 3 characteristics of a mammal. Which of these characteristics might improve a reptile's life?

Middle School

Give two reasons for the Battle of the Alamo. How might the outcome have been different had Houston arrived with extra Texas militia?

High School

Name 2 wars that have occurred in the past 100 years. Compare them. Find similarities and differences.

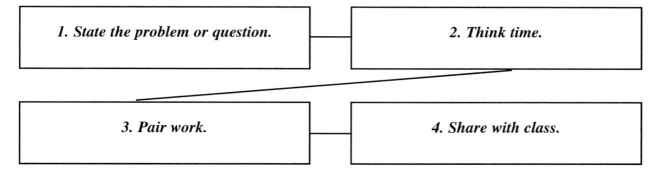

1. *State the problem or question.*   2. *Think time.*

3. *Pair work.*   4. *Share with class.*

Fact-or-Fiction

Fact-or-Fiction can be played in pairs or teams. It is a strategy designed for students to guess whether a statement is a fact or a fib. Pairs or teams are asked to create a hard-to-believe fact or a believable fib and announce it to the class. The other pairs or teams must guess whether the statement is a fact or a fib. Their answers can be shown in a number of different ways. Students can put their thumbs up for a fact or down for a fib. They can also write fact on the front of a piece of paper and fib on the back. Depending upon their answer, one side or the other is shown. This is a great strategy for pre-assessment, review, mastery or predicting.

Examples of Hard-to-Believe Facts:

- The strongest muscle in the body relative to its size is the tongue
- The woodpecker is able to move at 20 pecks a second!
- Some oak trees do not produce acorns until they are about 50 years old.
- Some turtles can breathe through their butts.
- The mockingbird is able to imitate the songs of 39 other species. It can also mimic other sounds, such as a piano or squeaky hinges.
- The nine-banded armadillo has identical quadruplets each time it gives birth.

Examples of Fiction Rumored to Be Facts:

- Coca-cola used to be green.
- The word *news* is an acronym formed from the words *north, east, west* and *south.*
- The word *golf* is an acronym formed from the words *gentlemen only, women forbidden.*

Toss-A-Question

This activity is sometimes called Snowball Fight. Toss-A-Question is a great way for review, for practicing skills, for making predictions, and other activities. Students write the required information on a piece of paper, wad it up and throw it at each other. The teacher allows this to go on for a specific amount of time. When time is called, students—individually, in pairs, or in teams—pick up the wads of paper and respond to the required information. This strategy is good to use when students seem restless after being in their seats too long. Playing Toss-A-Question allows them to get up and move around, yet still be involved in a learning situation. Below are examples of Toss-A-Question instructions that can be used with gifted students to promote higher-order thinking.

Elementary

Predict how the world would be different had the automobile not been invented.

Middle School

Create a solution to this problem: The world is full of trash with no place left to put it. What can be done?

High School

Where do you see the evolution of transportation in the future?

Stand and Share

This strategy involves team discussion of an issue and team members' subsequent sharing of their thoughts with the rest of the class. Teams are given a topic or issue to discuss. Each individual shares his or her thoughts with teammates. Once all team members feel they have an important idea to share about the issue, the whole team stands up. The teacher will ask one team member to share his or her thought. Once this is done, the teacher asks all students with similar ideas to sit down. Another student standing will be asked to share his or her idea.

The process is repeated until all students are seated. This technique does not take long, yet gives students the opportunity to have their ideas represented. (NOTE: If there are students who wish to share other ideas that have not been mentioned and if time permits, allow time at the end to accommodate those students.)

Find Someone Who…

This is a great way to pair up students with like interests or ideas. The teacher says, "Find someone who feels the same way as you about…." Students then move about the room searching for someone with the same idea. This can be done orally or written. It is also a good way to get to know classmates. Once each student has found a partner, the pairs discuss the issue and prepare to talk about it with other pairs. Often students are timid about expressing their ideas openly and individually. This strategy gives the students an ally. As the old saying goes, "There is safety in numbers."

EXAMPLES:

Elementary

Find Someone Who (enjoys science, math, social studies, language arts…; believes there is life in outer space; knows of a solution to the world's energy problems; etc.)

Middle School

Find Someone Who (plays football, basketball, soccer…; believes the world is on the verge of another ice age; plans to attend college; enjoyed a specific movie or book; etc.)

High School

Find Someone Who (believes there is a solution to world peace, hunger, religious persecution; wants to revise the economy in a different way; etc.)

Generating and Testing Hypotheses

Generating and testing hypotheses is one of the most powerful cognitive operations in learning and a great intervention strategy. Basically, it is application of knowledge. An example might be that after a student watches the demonstration of a microwave oven, he or she concludes that food can now be cooked in less than half the time it takes in a conventional oven. Another example might be that after a student watches the demonstration of how a can crusher works, the student concludes that using a can crusher allows more cans to fit in a recycling container.

Generating and testing hypotheses is the technique used to find solutions to many problems. Students use new learning, make a prediction based upon that learning, and test the prediction. Generating and testing hypotheses is usually associated with scientific theory; however, it can be used across the curriculum. Some areas in which this strategy can be used include system analysis, problem solving, historical investigation, inventions, experimental inquiry, and decision making. Activities that can be used to implement generating and testing hypotheses include Concept Attainment, Deductive/Inductive Thinking, Mystery Concept, and the 5 E's Lesson Design.

Concept Attainment

Concept attainment is a way to challenge students to formulate a concept through illustrations, word cards, or examples. The teacher selects a specific concept to be learned and defines its critical attributes. Positive and negative exemplars are then developed. As each is presented, it is identified as a positive exemplar or a negative one. As each exemplar is introduced, students are given time to think about it. The teacher continues to add exemplars asking students to give a sign (thumbs up, hands up, stand up) indicating that they have the concept. After a few students have gotten the concept, let those students take over the responsibility of identifying the exemplars as positive or negative. The teacher defines the attributes and announces the concept to those who did not guess it. A good example of this is prime numbers. Using the computer, create a Power Point slide that can add numbers, one by one, with no set order. As each is added, students try to guess the concept.

Concept attainment can be used to generate interest in a new idea, encourage predictions, pre-assess, review, or test for mastery. See an example of Concept attainment in E-17 . F-12 in Section V is a step-by-step resource for teachers and students to use in creating a concept-attainment lesson.

Deductive/Inductive Thinking

Deductive and inductive thinking are two methods of reasoning. Deductive thinking involves working from the general and moving towards the specific. Deductive reasoning is sometimes called a "top-down" approach. Inductive reasoning begins with a specific observation and broadens out to generalizations. It is often called the "bottom-up" approach. See the following diagram which gives a visual picture of deductive and inductive thinking.

DEDUCTIVE THINKING (top down)

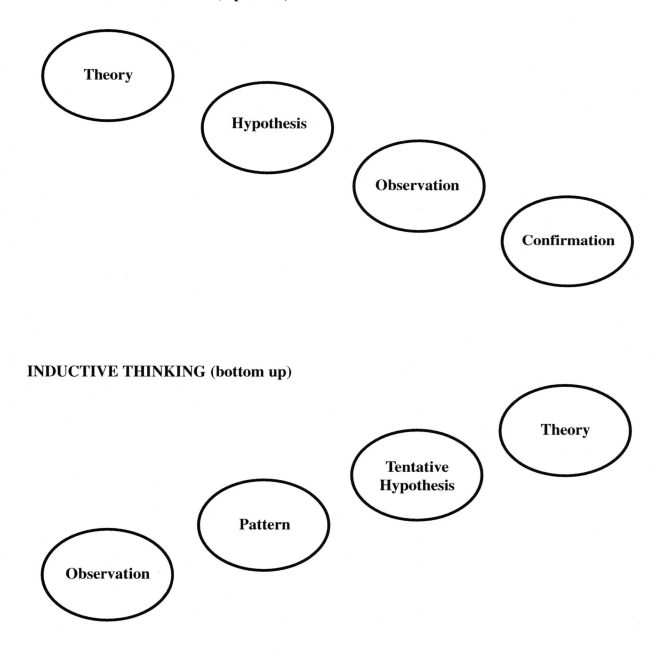

INDUCTIVE THINKING (bottom up)

See E-18 for an example of each.

Mystery Concept

Students are given a set of cards, each with a different attribute, yet all related to the same concept. The students are then asked to think about the cards and to group them under categories which they create. The students can move the cards around, changing categories and looking for common attributes among the cards until they can identify the mystery concept. The teacher can lead students to the categories by questioning, adding additional data, and giving cues and hints. See E-19 for Mystery Card Game examples. Blank Mystery Cards can be found in Section V, F-13.

5 E's Lesson Design

The 5 E's Lesson Design is another method of helping students generate and test a hypothesis. Each of the 5 E's is listed below with its purpose.

Engage: The <u>teacher</u> creates an exciting atmosphere about a topic to engage students in learning. The <u>students</u> define questions, decide upon tasks, make the connection from new to known, and define the relevance.

Explore: The <u>teacher</u> provides hands-on, minds-on activities for the students. At least two questions will be posed to encourage the students' exploration of the topic. The <u>students</u> become actively involved with the material. Teamwork is used to begin building a knowledge base.

Explain: The <u>teacher</u> asks two higher-order questions to solicit student explanations of the exploration. The teacher uses techniques that will help the students connect their exploration to the topic being studied. <u>Students</u> explain their discoveries, processes, and concepts that have been learned. This can be done through written, verbal or creative projects.

Elaborate: The <u>teacher</u> will develop students' understanding of the topic by using scientific terminology and showing application of the topic to daily living. <u>Students</u> expand their knowledge, make connections to similar concepts and apply the new learning to other situations.

Evaluate: The <u>teacher</u> checks for understanding through the development and use of rubrics, conducts student interviews, and monitors student projects. The <u>students</u> demonstrate their knowledge of the topic through portfolios, problem-based learning outputs and individual projects and products.

The 5 E's Lesson Design can be used across the curriculum. See E-20 for examples. A blank form can be found in Section V, F-14.

Venn Diagram

War

death

destruction

economic
hardships

weapons

Both

travel

government
intervention

environmental
issues

Peace

environmental issues
addressed

economic stability

industrial growth

© **Educational Impressions, Inc.** **73** *RTI for the Gifted Student*

RAINFOREST and DESERT

SIMILARITIES	DIFFERENCES
biomes	amounts of moisture
animals live in both	temperatures
plants live in both	plant species
plants used for medical research	animal species
	economy
	tourism
	human population

Sentence Frame

1. What do you know about <u>a grocery cart</u>?

2. I know that <u>a grocery cart</u> could be used in <u>a factory</u> because I learned in social studies that <u>products made in factories have to be moved to other departments</u>.

3. Explain another way that <u>a grocery cart</u> might be used.

<u>A grocery cart could also be used to move books around in a library</u>.

4. What might happen if the <u>grocery cart</u> did not exist?

<u>People would have a hard time getting their groceries into their vehicles</u>.

5. I suppose a motor could be added to the <u>grocery cart</u> to make a new <u>type of transportation for products</u>.

6. Other people, such as <u>the homeless</u>, could use the grocery cart for <u>transporting their belongings</u>.

Card Sort (Mammals/Reptiles)

protect young	most have claws
two-chambered heart	three- or four-chambered heart
marsupial	snake
elephant	not found in polar ice

Card Sort (Mammals/Reptiles)

warm blooded	cold blooded
fur	scales
babies born alive	most lay eggs
give milk	abandon young after birth

Card Sort (City/Rural)

| food crops | manufactured goods |

| village market | malls |

| 98% of United States | 2% of United States |

| irrigation | endless opportunities |

Card Sort (City/Rural)

peaceful	rush hour
farms	traffic
livestock	urbanized area
grass-roots America	high-rise apartments

Card Sort (Cell/Water)

mitosis	evaporation
prophase	condensation
metaphase	precipitation
prometaphase	collection

Card Sort (Cell/Water)

anaphase	sun
telophase	water vapor
reproduction	transportation
nucleus	clouds

Card Sort (Chemistry/Physics)

oxygen	force
water	velocity
acids	acceleration
bases	displacement

Card Sort (Chemistry/Physics)

ph scales	time
hydrogen	Newton's first law: inertia
bonding	momentum
mixtures	mass

Card Sort Answers

MAMMAL/REPTILE

Mammal	Reptile
warm blooded	cold blooded
fur	scales
babies born alive	most lay eggs
give milk	abandon young after birth
protect young	most have claws
two-chambered hear	three- or four-chambered heart
marsupial	snake
elephant	not found in polar ice

CITY/RURAL

City	Rural
peaceful	rush hour
farms	traffic
livestock	urbanized area
grass-roots America	high-rise apartments
food crops	manufactured goods
village market	malls
98% of United States	2% of United States
irrigation	endless opportunities

Card Sort Answers

CELL/WATER

Cell	Water
mitosis	evaporation
prophase	condensation
prometaphase	collection
metaphase	precipitation
anaphase	sun
telophase	water vapor
reproduction	transportation
nucleus	clouds

CHEMISTRY/PHYSICS

Chemistry	Physics
oxygen	force
water	velocity
acids	acceleration
bases	displacement
ph scales	time
hydrogen	Newton's first law: inertia
bonding	momentum
mixtures	mass

Concept Attainment

Design the Concept

Prime Numbers

List the Attributes

A. Number that can only be divided by itself and 1

B.

C.

D.

E.

Develop Positive and Negative Examples

POSITIVE	NEGATIVE
1. 11	**1.** six
2. 3	**2.** 14
3. 2	**3.** 9
4. seven	**4.** 4
5. 59	**5.** eight
6. five	**6.** 15
7. 31	**7.** twenty
8. 43	**8.** forty
9. seventy-three	**9.** 64
10. 83	**10.** 148

Concept Attainment, continued

Introduce the Process and Present the Examples

How: Draw two concentric circles on the board. Label one circle "Positive" and one "Negative." Begin to give examples to the students, writing the positive examples in the circle labeled "Positive" and negative ones in the circle labeled "Negative."

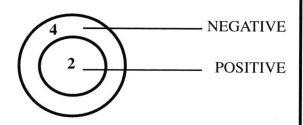

NEGATIVE

POSITIVE

Develop a Concept Definition

Definition: Let students put thumbs up when they know the concept. Students who know the concept can also give hints to those who do not have the concept.

Give More Examples if Needed

Discuss Process with Students and Evaluate Lesson

Evaluation: Explain the process to the students. Use colored cards for students to hold up during the game, keeping track of who understands the concept and who does not. A more formal evaluation measure can be used by giving students a paper/pencil test on prime numbers.

Encourage students to create their own concept-attainment lesson. These lessons can be used as an evaluation measure also.

Deductive/Inductive Thinking

Deductive Thinking

Theory: Natural disasters kill thousands of people each year.

Hypothesis: Tornados are more dangerous than hurricanes.

Observations: Information is gathered from data collected over a specific period of time as to how many deaths are caused by tornados and how many by hurricanes.

Confirmation: Data proves that more people are killed by tornados each year than by hurricanes.

Inductive Thinking

Observation: 350 people were killed by tornadoes in the United States during 2008.

Pattern: See the following graph for recorded tornado deaths from 2000 through 2007.

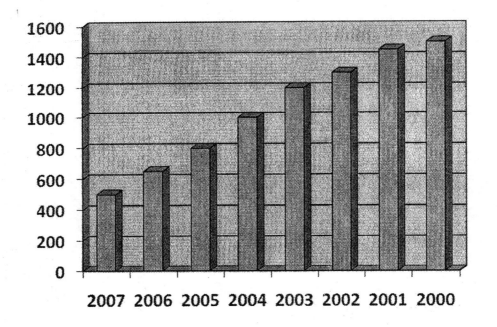

Tentative Hypothesis: The deaths by tornados dropped from 2000 to 2008 due to better warning systems.

Theory: Because technology has increased the ability to observe weather conditions that are conducive to tornado formations, weather experts can predict the tornado locations early enough to warn the public of danger.

Mystery Card Game (Plants)

food	water
stem	root
sun	photosynthesis
leaves	soil

Mystery Card Game (Middle East)

oil	desert
Iraq	Iran
Islam	coalition
Muslim	religious persecution

Mystery Card Game (American Civil War)

Gettysburg	North
South	General Lee
railroad	ships
slavery	Antietam

5 E's Lesson
Elementary Lesson: Plants

Engage:

The teacher divides students into groups of three or four and gives each team a copy of the Mystery Card Game about plants. After students have guessed the concept, teacher brings out several different plants for students to observe. The teacher presents information about what plants need to grow and the parts of a plant.

Explore

The teacher allows students to take plants from the soil and identify the parts. Students pose questions about what will happen if a plant does not have each of the elements deemed necessary for survival. Students form a hypothesis and set up experiments to test it. One plant will not have sun; another will have no water; and still another will have no soil. Students observe the plants and record the information.

Explain

Students present their findings.

Elaborate

Students use their observations to compare a plant to an animal. Students expand on the information by generating questions about human life.

Evaluate

The teacher checks students' understanding by using a rubric to grade the presentations and questions developed to further elaborate on the concept of life.

5 E's Lesson
Middle-School Integrated ELA, Math, Social Studies, Science Unit

Engage: The teacher offers the following scenario to students:

SCENARIO: A new middle school is being constructed. The students of the school see the architects' designs and determine that there will be enough space around the new building for parking without using an area in back of the building that contains several shade trees. Their idea is to create a space for all students for daily exercise, organized sports, and pick-up games.

Explore: The teacher suggests the following areas of exploration. Students will petition the administration and local board of education for their desired use of the space. Teacher and students together determine that the solution to their problem will include a scale-model playground using the U.S. customary measurement system or the metric system. The purpose of the model is to exemplify learning for an authentic audience and to accommodate rigor in learning as they analyze, synthesize, and evaluate their knowledge, comprehension, and application.

The problem includes <u>issues</u> of health and safety. Students explore safety issues and determine the placement of playground equipment, such as tetherball, a volleyball court, and a croquet field.

Students integrate a study of native plants <u>(science)</u> to determine which plants are native to their area and placement of the plants in their space.

<u>Topics</u> demonstrated and integrated into the unit include Measurement (Math), Safety (Health & Physical Education), Technology (Technological applications), and Writing (English Language Arts).

<u>Facts</u> in the following areas support students' knowledge and skills to address the theory, concept, and products of the unit include metric or U.S. measurement units; measuring length, area and perimeter; drawing to scale (ratio); area to be used; needs of playground users; types of playground equipment; technical writing; and persuasive writing.

Explain: Students will prepare a formal presentation for the administration and local board of education. The presentation will include a written plan for the area, a scale model, blueprints, and explanation of the overall plan. It will also include a PowerPoint presentation with movie maker.

Elaborate: If the students' plan is accepted, students will be divided into groups according to their area of interest and expertise to initiate the plan.

If the students' plan is not accepted, they will adjust the plan to meet specifications stated by administrators and local board of education, develop a new plan, or find an area to accomplish their original goals within the community instead of on school property.

Evaluate: Students will be evaluated by rubric on each step of the development of their plan. Comments by administrators and the board members will also be considered. Students will critique their plan before and after presentation for strengths and weaknesses.

Section III

Classroom Management Strategies for Differentiation

- Curriculum Compacting
- Tiered Assignments
- Interest Centers/Interest Groups
- Learning Stations
- Agendas
- Exit Cards
- Learning Contracts

Classroom Management Strategies

Classroom management techniques offer a wide variety of intervention strategies that allow gifted students to address areas of interest and new learning while the teacher meets the needs of other students in the room. Classroom management techniques accommodate RTI for the gifted student by offering methods that help the teacher to determine if students require learning time with other advanced learners or time with independent study, Tiers II and III.

This section addresses the following management techniques:

- Curriculum Compacting
- Tiered Assignments
- Interest Centers or Interest Groups
- Learning Stations
- Agendas
- Exit Cards
- Learning Contracts

There are a variety of classroom management methods that may be found in the literature related to gifted learners.* Some examples are anchor activities, choice boards, group investigations, library cards, and menus. All are appropriate interventions that meet the needs of gifted learners through learning options and to meet requirements of a diverse classroom.

*See Marzano, R., J. Pickering and J. Pollack (2001). *Classroom Instruction that Works.* Association for supervision and Curriculum Development. Alexandria, VA.

Connection to RTI for the Gifted Student

Curriculum Compacting

Alternative intervention activities suggested with curriculum compacting offer insight into skills and abilities of the gifted student(s). Pre-assessment provides the teacher with information about the needs of the students:

- Do the gifted need to remain at Tier I with all students?
- Should they be grouped with other students who have similar abilities in order to complete an alternative assignment?
- Should the student(s) be given time to work on an independent study related to the content?

Tiered Assignments

In a heterogeneous class a teacher uses varied levels of activities, tiered assignments, to ensure that students explore ideas and learn content at a level that builds on their prior knowledge and offers opportunities for continued growth. Tiered assignments offer opportunities for students at Tiers I, II, and III. Students may begin their learning with whole-class instruction (Tier I) and proceed to tiered assignment that will accommodate Tiers II and/or III. Tiered assignment maximize learning by focusing students on the content at individual levels of challenge.

Interest Centers or Interest Groups

Gifted students pursue content at greater depth when given time and opportunity to explore their interests. Work in interest centers and with interest groups in Tier II accommodates their learning nature and needs.

Learning Stations

Learning Stations are used in ways similar to those of Interest Centers/Interest Groups.

Agendas

Agendas are designed for use after students are pre-assessed for compacting. Teachers create agendas for Tiers II and III of RTI.

Exit Cards

Exit Cards are intended as a means for the teacher to assess learning. The assessment will determine if students remain at Tier I of RTI or move to Tier II or III.

Learning Contracts

Contracts are used when gifted students are working in Tiers II and III. Contracts are a classroom-management strategy because they free the teacher to work with other students while the gifted are engaged and because they offer gifted students the opportunity to work on appropriate curriculum while developing independent study skills.

Curriculum Compacting: Tiers I, II and III

What Is Compacting?

Compacting is a process in which the teacher assesses students prior to teaching a new skill or new content to determine what they know, what they do not know, and what alternative experiences (Tiers II and III) will replace those activities designed for content already mastered (Tier I).

Curriculum compacting streamlines and modifies grade-level curriculum by eliminating material that students have previously learned. This process challenges the students and offers time for differentiated enrichment or acceleration activities to students who demonstrate high levels of achievement.

Benefits for G/T Students

Compacting…

- recognizes the large reservoir of knowledge;
- satisfies the students' hunger to delve more deeply into topics as well as to learn about additional topics;
- encourages independence in thought and action; and
- eliminates boredom and lethargy resulting from repetition of information already learned and unnecessary drill and practice.

Compacting offers the student the opportunity to develop in ways that accommodate learning needs and the offers the teacher a chance to create learning experiences of greater depth and breadth.

Who Can Benefit? Consider the twins: Early-finisher Elena and Never-finished Nathan.

- Elena consistently finishes her work early. It is done well and correctly. She consistently thinks and expresses her thoughts in a more advanced way than her peers. Often she asks the teacher if she can study the topic in a different way or look deeper into the ideas. Elena is motivated to do her work and consistently performs at a high level. When she finishes her work, she may create her own puzzles or games.

- The opposite of Elena is her twin, never-finished Nathan. Nathan possesses many of the same abilities as Elena, but he procrastinates. It appears that Nathan is either a perfectionist who finds it difficult to reach an end because of his need to make the assignment perfect or he is a procrastinator who does not wish the teacher to know of his hidden abilities. If the teacher determines whether it is perfectionism or procrastination that causes Nathan to lag with finishing his work, she can accommodate his learning needs, and he will be willing to show his true capabilities.

Both of the twins can profit from curriculum compacting. Elena will be able to move forward from facts and ideas she already knows or can grasp easily, while Nathan can find areas of interest to develop at his pace because of the extra time created through compacting. If he has the time to work, the teacher will be able to determine if perfectionism or procrastination is interfering with his ability to finish work.

When provided the opportunity to move forward through the curriculum at a faster pace, gifted students will accept the challenge to delve more deeply into the subject and/or to learn in more complex ways.

Types of Compacting

There are two types of compacting: basic skills and content. Basic skills include tasks that students routinely complete in drill-and-practice sessions. Examples are spelling, math computation, and basic grammar skills in ELA. Pre-assessment can determine the students' level of expertise with basic skills.

The second type of compacting relates to the content. Core content areas can be compacted as can strands within each content. Often students know a great deal about the subject or can learn it very quickly through reading or practice that is based on higher-order thinking.

The Process

- Establish outcomes for the unit or the defined instruction.
- Identify students who may benefit from compacting or offer the opportunity to all students (use as a diagnostic tool).
- Develop the pre-assessment.*
- Determine what content can and cannot be compacted. (See How to Compact.)
- Establish a system for compacting the basic skills and/or content (Tier I)
- Develop acceleration strategies and/or enrichment activities for students who will receive the compacted basic skills and/or content. (Tiers II and III)
- Develop a means of keeping records about the pre-assessment and about the work students complete in compacted basic skills and/or content.

*Some teachers inform students of pre-assessment opportunities several days in advance. This allows the students time with the content or skills. If they already know the material, they will be ready for the assessment. If not, they may be given the choice of learning the material on their own in order to free time for alternative activities.

How to Compact

When considering what and how to compact for your students, determine the following about your unit or content:

1. What's important? What are the big ideas in this unit? What do I want the students to know when the unit is complete?

2. What can be skipped or eliminated? Are there facts or portions of the content that are not critical to #1?

3. What do students already know? and/or What are students already able to do? Make plans to determine what previous knowledge the students bring. What ideas or tasks do the students know at an expert level?

4. Use the answers from #3 to determine the following: What will students grasp easily? What can be accomplished quickly? How quickly can they learn the concepts and/or skills not already known? What can be assigned and assumed to be learned without spending class time on the ideas or tasks?

Considerations

Some considerations and procedures to be provided for the students before beginning the process:

- Explain the process and its benefits to all students.
- Provide the pre-assessment to determine what students have mastered and what they still need to know about the skills or content in the chapter/unit. Document all pre-assessment.
- Allow students to choose the activities they will participate in during their compacting.
- Prepare a written plan and timeline for accelerated/enrichment study.

Planning Alternative Activities (Tiers II and III)

When planning alternative activities, consider the following:

- What do students need to know?
- What do students need to do?
- How do students react to content? (What is their level of interest?)

Teachers may set their own expectations, but these are some possible guidelines:

- Students must take all chapter/unit quizzes and must maintain a 90% or better or at least a 4 on a 5-point rubric.
- Students must choose to participate in the compacting activity(ies).
- Students may choose to opt out of compacting at any time.

Use curriculum compacting to meet the needs of your gifted learners while providing time for work with other students. See E-21 for a compacted lesson. F-15 in Section V is a blank curriculum-compacting form.

Tiered Assignments: Tiers I, II and III

What Are Tiered Assignments?

Tiered assignments begin with a determination of outcomes for learning. What activities will offer students a chance to learn and illustrate their learning? In a differentiated classroom, a teacher uses varied levels of tasks to ensure that students explore ideas and use skills at a level that builds on what they already know and encourages growth. Activities may include levels of challenge or complexity or they may be built on learning styles. Tiering of assignments by learning styles is based on learning preference as offered by Howard Gardner in his description of multiple intelligences. Tiering of assignments by challenge or complexity is related to the levels of intellectual behavior as described by Benjamin Bloom.

Use Bloom's Taxonomy as a guide to develop tasks at various challenge levels. By keeping the content focus of the activity the same, but providing activities at varying degrees of difficulty, the teacher ensures that students are appropriately challenged and that they come away with key skills and understandings. When tiered by complexity, varied tasks are provided that address a student's level of readiness—from introductory levels to more abstract, less concrete, advanced work. Be careful to provide *advanced* work to higher-level students rather than just *more* work.

With tiered assignments all students focus on outcomes determined by the teacher, but these outcomes are offered at differing levels of complexity. While students work at varied degrees of difficulty on their tasks, they all explore the same essential ideas and work at different levels of thought. Activities for gifted learners are more abstract and open ended. Groups eventually come together to share and learn from each other.

Look for TIC-TAC-TOE, Menus, and Levels of Tiered Assignment. See E-22 for examples of tiered lessons. F-16 in Section V provides a blank form for writing a tiered assignment.

Caution! Tiered assignments should…

- be *different* work, not simply more or less work;
- be equally active and engaging;
- be equal across levels in terms of work expectations and time needed; and
- require the use of key concepts and skills.

Tiered Assignment Process

- Select a concept and determine if the tiered assignment will be built on challenge, complexity, or learning style.
- Pre-assess students for the appropriate level of assignment. (Tier I)
- Create a variety of activities and rubrics to evaluate the challenge, complexity, and/or learning style of those activities.
- Match students to the appropriate tiered assignments. (Tiers II and III)

Considerations: Teachers must remember the following for Tiers II and III for gifted learners:

- Use advanced materials.
- Ensure complexity of thought.
- Make certain that students transform ideas, not merely reproduce them.
- Make activities open ended.
- Allow exploration and application of content.
- Encourage broader reading than for average learners.
- Focus on problem solving.
- Provide meaningful work with peers of similar interest and readiness.
- Develop creative abilities.

Interest Centers or Interest Groups: Tiers I, II and III

What are Interest Centers or Interest Groups?

Interest centers for younger students and interest groups for older students provide enrichment for students who can demonstrate mastery with required work. Content is built around enrichment that adds depth and complexity to students' learning. Learning includes opportunities to explore content in an area of interest. For example, centers/groups may be divided into categories such as the following to peak students' interest: story center, design center, performance center, reflection center, test center, and reasoning center. See E-23 for examples of Tic-Tac-Toe Activities and Learning (Interest) Center activities. F-17 of Section V provides a blank form.

Purpose for G/T Students: Interest centers and groups...

- provide opportunity for study in greater breadth and depth of topics found in the regular curriculum;
- allow for introduction of topics not in the regular curriculum;
- can satisfy students' curiosity and allow them to explore the "hows" and "whys" of things;
- allow for student choice; and
- draw on ability to make connections between topics.

Process: The following criteria are required for positive outcomes with centers/groups:

- Tasks must be suitably complex for a high-ability learner.
- Students of like interests should be able to work together.
- The gifted learner should be involved in the research and creation of the interest centers and of the interest-group tasks.
- Centers should be changed less often, calling for more depth in fewer topics.

Considerations

- Centers should provide work that requires higher-level thinking.
- Groups should be responsible for their learning through agendas or contracts.

Learning Stations: Tiers I, II and III

What are Learning Stations?

Learning stations are collections of materials learners use to explore topics or to practice skills. For gifted learners, learning stations should move beyond cursory exploration of topics and practice of basic skills and should provide study in greater breadth and depth on topics of interest.

Learning Stations should offer different kinds of activities to reach students with varied interests and can be planned in a variety of ways. Stations allow choice based on interests and ability and provide an outlet for creativity. Students may choose which station to go to first. Students will go through all stations in a set amount of time (class period, week, end of unit).

Benefits for G/T Students

Learning Stations…

- draw on advanced thinking skills,
- provide for continuous development of students' skills,
- draw on advanced reading skills,
- allow for student independence, and
- develop advanced skills in research and technology.

Process

Stations are different from centers in that each station is connected to one concept. For example, one writing station may include persuasive writing, another may focus on narrative writing, still another on explanatory writing, and so on. A math station may describe a math process with practice and problem solving related to that process.

Group gifted students into clusters. Assign them one of the stations or allow the cluster to choose the station. (Tier II)

Considerations

- Offer some tasks that require transformation and application.
- Monitor what students do and learn at the centers.
- Balance student and teacher choices about stations.

Agendas: Tier III

What are Agendas?

Agendas offer students a personalized list of tasks to complete in a specified time. Student agendas are similar to those that are used to organize meetings. Students receive their agenda when they enter the room and complete it during the class period, the day, or the time period specified on the document. Agendas help students to organize their time and tasks.

Considerations

Make certain the agendas…

- facilitate organizational skills,
- encourage independence in learning,
- focus students on goals, and
- allow for freedom of choice based on needs and interests.

Sample Agenda

Agenda

Name	**Date**

I.   Complete one (1) activity in TIC-TAC-TOE.

II. Add to bibliography for research project.

III. Begin work on _____ interest center.

IV. Turn in completed work and indicate with rationale which activities have been tabled for a later time.

Exit Cards: Tiers I, II and III

What are Exit Cards?

The teacher gives each student an index card at the end of instruction or at the end of the class period. Students respond to a pre-determined prompt on their index card and then turn it in as they leave the classroom or move to another subject. The teacher reviews the responses and separates the cards into Tiers I, II, and III based on preset criteria.

Purpose of Exit Cards

Exit Cards serve as formative assessment. They are designed to determine if students understand the concept or skill and if they are ready to move to another level in RTI.

Examples

Elementary

All students: Name the parts of a cell.

G/T students: How are parts of a cell like a _____? (The students create a comparison.)

Secondary

All students: List three characteristics of two characters you read about.

G/T students: Write the name of one character from each of two stories that you read. List three characteristics that are common to both.

Learning Contracts: Tier III

What are Contracts?

Contracts take a number of forms. All begin with an agreement between the student and the teacher. The teacher offers choices about how a student will complete tasks and confers with the student about how to accomplish the tasks. The student agrees to use the freedoms appropriately in designing and completing work according to specifications. The student; the teacher, the parent(s) or guardian(s); and, when appropriate, the administrator(s) sign the contract. Contracts may be renegotiated with approval of all signees.

Purpose of the Contract: The contract...

- eliminates the need for unnecessary skills work;
- makes skills more relevant by integrating them into high-interest tasks;
- draws on the curiosity and develops the independence of the student; and
- allows for advanced and extended study on topics of interest.

Considerations

- Make the contract specific enough to include a time line for completion.
- Do not make skills work the centerpiece of the contract. Focus on concepts or problems with skills integrated into the products.
- Establish clear and rigorous standards for success at the outset.

SAMPLE CONTRACT

G/T Program 2010-2011

This is a contract between Moore High School and _____.

Student's Name

The terms of the contract are as follows:

    In order to receive one-half credit for Career Connections, State Standard # 127.12, and one-half credit for Video Technology, State Standard # 126.27, the student must meet all of the following criteria:

- Complete all State Standards for Career Connections.
- Complete all State Standards for Video Technology.
- Observe nurses and make observations of the way they work.
- Combine Video Technology and Career Connections to give an in-depth look into the nursing profession.

<u>Mrs. Dwayne</u> will be my mentor and facilitating teacher for Career Connections.

<u>Mrs. Karlo</u> will be my mentor and facilitating teacher for Video Technology.

    The results of this study will be assessed on the basis of the seriousness of the approach to the study, the degree of critical thinking achieved, and the effectiveness and appropriateness of the product. The student will perform a periodic evaluation as well as a final evaluation based on state standards at the end of the term.

    This contract must be signed by the student, the parents, the principal, the G/T instructor and any facilitating teacher/mentor involved.

_____   _____

Student   Parent/Guardian

_____   _____

Facilitating Teacher   Principal

_____   _____

G/T Instructor   Mentor

_____   _____

Mentor   Other

Compacting (Grades 5–8)
Unit: Texas History   Type: Content

Demonstrated Mastery	Documentation
Standards: • Points of reference: Texas history • Explain the impact of the U.S. Constitution on the writing of the Texas Constitution. **Concepts and Skills:** • Reading and interpreting text • Drawing conclusions based on analysis of the U.S. & Texas constitutions	**Pre-assessment:** • End of unit benchmark text

Needs for Further Instruction	Procedures and Resources
• In-depth information about events that influenced the U.S. & Texas constitutions • Exploration of the ideas of writers of both constitutions regarding freedom	Date: _____ Independent Study Date: _____ Class Discussion and Quiz Date: _____ Complete Independent Study

Replacement Task	Resources
• Read a nonfiction book or a biography about one of the writers of the Texas constitution. • Develop a first-person oral presentation. The class will interview you as a writer of the Texas Constitution.	• Library • Internet • Historical Society • State Capital

Tiered Lesson (Grades 4–8)
Unit:Enigmas

Objectives:
1. Students will develop an understanding of enigmas by researching several different ones.
2. Students will generate and test hypothesis about the existence of the enigma.

Whole-class Activities	**Assessment**
Break into teams of 3 or 4 students to research the Marfa Lights.	It includes all students.
Teams present their theories of the existence of the Marfa Lights.	The presentation is well organized. Insightful theories are presented.

Level 1 Activity	**Assessment**
Use resources to research the Marfa Lights.	At least 4 theories are researched.
Make a list of the theories about their existence.	The theories are accurate.

Level 2 Activity	**Assessment**
Research different branches of science.	All branches are present.
Create a chart of the branches related to the theories and place each theory under the appropriate branch of science.	The chart is clear and correct.

Level 3 Activity	**Assessment**
Choose one theory and generate a hypothesis about its truth.	The steps are complete and accurate.
Create an experiment to test the hypothesis.	The experiment design is valid.
Present the results to the class.	The presentation is well organized. The information is correct.

Whole-class Culminating Activities
Each team presents the results of their experiment to the class.

Each student will draw his or her own conclusions regarding the theory's accuracy based upon the results of his or her team's experiment. These findings will be recorded in a journal.

Student-choice Activity: Animal Tic-Tac-Toe

Standards/Objectives: Use research skills to learn about the animal. Create products that reflect what is learned.

1. **Create a scrapbook about the animal's life.**	**2.** **Write a poem about the animal.**	**3.** **Write a story about the animal.**
4. **Draw a diagram of the animal. Label unique parts of the animal.**	**5.** **Make a fact file of important facts about the animal.**	**6.** **Create a 3-D graphic organizer using the note-card information from your research.**
7. **Design a habitat for the animal that might be found in a zoo. Label the illustration.**	**8.** **Create a foldable book about the animal.**	**9.** **Design a bookmark with facts about the animal.**

I/we chose the following activities: No. _____, No._____, and No._____.

Name(s): _____

Due dates: _____, _____, and _____

Student-choice Activity: George Washington Tic-Tac-Toe

Standards/Objectives: Use research skills to learn about George Washington. Create products that reflect what is learned.

1. Design a scrapbook that tells the story of George Washington's life.	**2.** Create a 3-D graphic organizer using your research about Washington.	**3.** Write a speech Washington might have made encouraging the British to give Americans their independence.
4. Create a travel brochure that shows the many areas Washington mapped.	**5.** Write a poem about Washington's life.	**6.** Create a mural that shows important events in Washington's life.
7. Design a book jacket and bookmark that creatively present facts about Washington.	**8.** Write a story about George Washington's life. Create a book using your story.	**9.** Write a newspaper article about Washington becoming the first President.

I/we chose the following activities: No. _____, No._____, and No._____.

Name(s): _____

Due dates: _____, _____, and _____

Student-choice Activity: Middle-grade U.S. History Tic-Tac-Toe

Standards/Objectives: Use research skills to learn about United States history. Create products that reflect what is learned.

1.	2.	3.
Create a song or rap that describes the reasons colonists chose to come to the English colonies. Present your original work for an audience.	You represent slaves in their fight for freedom from slave merchants. Present an argument describing why you and your people should be returned to Africa.	Research and create an original painting or drawing showing what life was like in one of the original thirteen colonies.
4.	**5.**	**6.**
Create and publish a brochure encouraging American colonists to join the Continental Army. Use persuasive language and include some type of illustration or graphic.	Write and produce a play about the Second Continental Congress. Show how delegates came to agree to declare independence and to sign the document. Include important facts.	Produce and videotape a news interview with one of the Patriots of the Revolution.
7.	**8.**	**9.**
Suppose you were asked to design a coin for the new government. Illustrate your coin. Then describe it and explain why you designed it as you did.	Write your own version of a Bill of Rights for your school. Be sure that you can give educated reasons to support your Bill of Rights.	Write a letter to the newspaper that explains why a new constitution is needed for the thirteen states that formed after the American Revolution.

I/we chose the following activities: No. _____, No._____, and No._____.

Name(s): _____

Due dates: _____, _____, and _____

Student-choice Activity: *Courage* Tic-Tac-Toe

Standards/Objectives: Use novels, short stories, nonfiction, plays, print and visual media and research skills to learn create a Courage Diary and a modern Profile of Courage. Explore courage across the ages and cite examples of courage you observe in the modern world to create a definition of what you believe to be true courage.

1.	2.	3.
Create a Courage Diary. Record all examples of courage that you find and tell where you find them: at home, at school, on the news in literature, in texts, in music… everywhere! Cite sources.	**Analyze your diary to decide what society believes about courage. Based on trends and patterns in history, what are the principles on which courage is based?**	**Compare society's beliefs about courage with your own beliefs using a Venn Diagram.**
4.	**5.**	**6.**
Based on society's definition and your own ideas, develop criteria that you will use to evaluate whether an act or person is truly courageous.	**Describe a person or an act that would <u>not</u> be considered courageous by most of society but might be seen as courageous from different perspective.**	**Create your own definition of *courage* and *courageous*.**
7.	**8.**	**9.**
Provide an example of a person or an act that best exemplifies your own definition of *courage* or *courageous*. Explain why.	**Explain the importance of the study of what it means to be courageous. How might your study change you or your audience?**	**Present your definition or findings using 1 of these methods:** **Video-recorded interview** **Audio-recorded reflections** **Photographs with captions** **A computer presentation** **An art show** **Original song**

I/we chose the following activities: No. _____, No._____, and No._____.

Name(s): _____

Due dates: _____, _____, and _____

Section III

Products and Their Assessment

Products and Their Assessment

Tier III of the Response to Intervention Pyramid involves an independent study project that results in a product. Tier III is the highest level of intervention represented and should be required of all gifted students. This is the area in which gifted students who have been taught higher-order thinking and processing skills are equipped with the strategies needed to produce a product of professional quality.

Creating a product is a very important part of your students' education, but the ability to produce quality products does not come naturally. Students must be taught the necessary skills. These skills should be addressed at an early age, preferably beginning in kindergarten. If students have this training early, by the time they are in high school most will understand the requirements of professional products and produce such.

What Is a Product?

In order to teach the skills, one must understand what a product is and what is required to create a product. A product is defined as "a vehicle for communicating information and/or demonstrating skills for specific purposes to authentic audiences." It can be anything that is created which reflects the learned information in some way. For students in early grades, a product is a way to present their research in a creative way. For older grades, a product is a way to solve a problem in a unique way by fully understanding the topic through in-depth research. By exposing students to this high level of learning, educators are building a foundation and setting the stage for them to experience success in college and future careers.

Reasons for a Product

In order to teach the skills, one must understand what a product is and what is required to create a professional product. A product may be used as…

- the end result of an assignment or unit,
- a vehicle for communication,
- a way to demonstrate skills, and
- an assignment with a future.

Products do not always have to be a research paper. Students often lose interest in a project if they are required to write a research paper. There are other ways for students to show what they have learned from their research other than writing a paper; nevertheless, some educators feel that every research project must include one. If you are one of those educators, perhaps a short paper could be required to accompany other types of projects.

Benefits of producing a product. Products…

- engage students in hands-on, minds-on learning experiences;
- motivate students;
- allow students to make authentic connections;
- require higher-level thinking and problem solving;
- allow for and encourage self-expression and creativity;
- foster pride in one's work;
- are relevant beyond the classroom;
- help develop lifelong learners; and
- are an effective way to differentiate.

Independent studies that require products are also an excellent way to help high-school students decide upon a career. As students study topics that may lead to future careers, they gain a deeper understanding of that area of interest. Here is an example of when a student's product choice and research led to a change in her choice of future career:

> I had a high-school student who wanted to become a pediatrician. Her independent study was on the topic of pediatrics. I arranged for her to shadow my family medical doctor. After attending the delivery of several babies, both natural and c-section, the student came to me one day and said, "Mrs. Carlile, please don't be upset with me, but I have decided that being a pediatrician is not for me." I'm sure that her parents were very happy that she made that choice *before* attending medical school. This saved her parents an enormous amount of money, and her, several years of unnecessary college work. She has since decided to become a teacher. What a great career!

This young lady did create a product resulting from her study of pediatrics. She developed a brochure that included all the different fields of pediatrics and the education needed to specialize in each field. Copies of the brochure were placed in the guidance counselor' s office to use with high-school students in making career choices. The next year she developed a children's book that could be given to children going through the minor surgery of having tubes implanted in their ears. She made several copies and gave them to the doctor to use with his patients.

The following is an example of when a student's product led to a deeper love of the topic and reinforced his desire to pursue a career in that field:

> A young man in my high-school class wanted to build a potato shooter that used pneumatics as its power source. He began the project by researching penny shooters, which led to his creation of one. He continued his research until the potato shooter was completed. This led to his use of engineering principals in the creation of a T-shirt shooter that could be used at football and basketball games. The T-shirt shooter was used by the cheerleaders to shoot spirit shirts into the crowd. He continued to experiment with the shooter until he designed a pneumatic power source.

This young man's research and hands-on work with his product led to an appreciation for engineering that stayed with him. He applied to and was accepted into the Air Force Academy and graduated with an engineering degree. His ability to participate in the independent study and to develop a product helped him gain acceptance into the Air Force Academy. This ability will likely help him in whatever future career he undertakes as well, for products fulfill a societal need.

How to Get Started

In order to achieve quality products, the following issues need to be considered:

- Instructional intent
- Time
- Expense
- Assessment

Instructional Intent: First the educator must ask, "What is the purpose of doing the study and the reason for creating the product?" The teacher must decide if the product is a reflection of the new learning, a creative solution to a problem, or an experience that leads to future learning.

Time: Next the educator needs to consider how much time can be spent on a product. If it takes three weeks for a student to create a product and the unit is to be taught for only two weeks, then the product is too time consuming. The product choices given by the teacher must be in line with the amount of time to be spent on the unit.

Expense: Expenses must also be considered. Most schools do not have a budget that allows the luxury of expensive products. This is not usually a problem with younger students; however, with older students, the products become more elaborate and more costly. Funds will be needed for product production. Depending upon the policy of the school board, students may be required to pay for the supplies needed to complete their product.

Assessment: The teacher must decide upon the type of assessment to be used. There are many ways to assess a product. Some assessments, such as the Texas Performance Standards Project, use numbers with the criteria. Scores range from 1 to 5, depending upon the grade level. Other types of rubrics can also be used. See E-24 for examples of assessment rubrics.

When assessing a product-oriented unit of study, the following need to be addressed:

- What did the student learn about the content?
- What did the student learn about him/herself as the learner?
- How much innovation and creativity was put into the learning and presentation?
- What is the learner ready to learn next?

Once these questions have been considered, a plan is created for the unit. See E-25 for an example of a unit plan. A blank unit plan can be found in Section V, F-18.

Students must understand the guidelines for the product development and be aware of the assessment measure that will be used to assess the unit. The teacher should provide students with a list of products that include all learning styles. (Refer to Section I, Research, for more information.)

With younger students, it is best to supply a list of four product choices. When they are given a long list, such as the one found in E-26, it is often hard for them to narrow the list down to one product. They tend to want to do all the products. Products that fit into the field of study are the best ones to use. Be sure to address the four issues: intent, time, expense, and assessment.

Quality Products

Students must be taught how to produce quality products. The components of quality products include the following:

- Content
- Plan
- Presentation
- Creativity
- Reflection

Content: Content refers to *what* you want the student to learn. The information presented in the product must be accurate and thorough. It should include complexity of thought, including recall, skill/concept, strategic thinking, and extended thinking. The product should be well organized.

Plan: Students should plan the product before creating it. Products benefit when students think through the materials needed, the steps to complete it, and how they want the finished product to look. See E-27 for a sample product plan. A blank plan sheet can be found in Section V, F-19.

Presentation: The presentation of learning within the product is important for credibility. If the product includes written aspects, then the text, graphics, layout, plan, purpose, and illustration should be neat and accurate. If the presentation is oral, the product should be well organized and should include vocabulary of the discipline and should be clearly presented.

Creativity: The product should be innovative and should include some unique ideas. Higher-order thinking—Bloom's levels of analysis, synthesis, and evaluation—should be incorporated into the product. The product should also exhibit levels of creativity, such as those described by E. Paul Torrance: fluency, flexibility, originality, and elaboration. A high-quality product, especially with the older students, should include varying perspectives or differing points of view.

Reflection: Once the product has been completed, the student should reflect on the learning. Questions posed about the learning and product might include the following:

- What did I learn about the content by completing my product?
- What connections did I make?
- Did I include depth and complexity in my product?
- How much effort did I include in my product?
- Where will this learning lead me?

A blank product self-reflection form can be found in Section V, F-20.

Game Board Rubric

Name: _____ Date: _____

	POINTS	Absent	NSH*	Good	Excellent	
		0	1	2	3	4
C	**Board** • Neat • Uniform spaces • Relevant to topic • Legible					
R	**Markers** • Appropriate size • Distinguishable • User friendly					
I						
T	**Directions** • Clear • Easy to follow					
E						
R	**Content** • Accurate • Enhances knowledge • Comprehensive					
I						
A	**Mechanics** • Correct spelling, • Correct grammar • Correct punctuation					
	POINTS					

*NSH = Needs Some Help

TOTAL POINTS: _____
Grade: _____
Comments:
_____
_____
_____
_____
_____
_____

Grade

16–20 = A
12–15 = B
9–11 = C
6–8 = D
0–5 = F

Pamphlet/Brochure Rubric

Name:_____   Date: _____

		Absent	NSH*	Good	Excellent	
	POINTS	0	1	2	3	4
C R I T E R I A	**Front Cover** • Clear • Relevant to topic • Eye-catching					
	Mechanics • Correct spelling • Appropriate grammar • Correct punctuation					
	Content • Accurate • Enhances knowledge • Comprehensive					
	Graphics • Neat • Colorful • Relevant to topic					
	Back Cover • Resources listed • Contact information					
	POINTS					

*NSH = Needs Some Help

TOTAL POINTS: _____
Grade: _____
Comments:

_____
_____
_____
_____
_____

Grade

16–20 = A
12–15 = B
9–11 = C
6–8 = D
0–5 = F

Poem Rubric

Name:_____ Date: _____

		Absent	NSH*	Good	Excellent	
	POINTS	0	1	2	3	4
C	**Topic** • Relevant to topic					
R **I**	**Words** • Vocabulary from subject • Creative use of words					
T **E**	**Rhythm** • Clear • Poem type apparent • Theme apparent					
R **I**	**Mechanics** • Correct spelling • Correct grammar • Correct punctuation					
A	**Illustrations** • Relevant to topic • Neat					
	POINTS					

*NSH = Needs Some Help

TOTAL POINTS: _____
Grade: _____
Comments:
_____
_____
_____
_____
_____
_____

Grade

16–20 = A
12–15 = B
9–11 = C
6–8 = D
0–5 = F

Pop-up Book Rubric

Name:_____ Date: _____

		Absent	NSH*	Good	Excellent	
	POINTS	0	1	2	3	4
C R I T E R I A	**Pop-ups** • Workable • Neat • Relevant to topic					
	Creativity • Unique ideas • Original					
	Story Structure • Beginning • Middle • End					
	Mechanics • Correct spelling • Correct sentence structure • Correct punctuation					
	Appearance • Neat • Has eye appeal • Illustrations and colors well planned					
	POINTS					

*NSH = Needs Some Help

TOTAL POINTS: _____
Grade: _____
Comments:
_____
_____
_____
_____
_____
_____

Grade

16-20 = A
12-15 = B
9-11 = C
6-8 = D
0-5 = F

Poster Rubric

Name:_____ Date: _____

		Absent	NSH*	Good	Excellent	
	POINTS	0	1	2	3	4
C R I T E R I A	**Pop-ups** • Workable • Neat • Relevant to topic					
	Creativity • Unique ideas • Original					
	Story Structure • Beginning • Middle • End					
	Mechanics • Correct spelling • Correct sentence structure • Correct punctuation					
	Appearance • Neat • Has eye appeal • Illustrations and colors well planned					
	POINTS					

*NSH = Needs Some Help

TOTAL POINTS: _____
Grade: _____
Comments:
_____
_____
_____
_____
_____
_____

Grades

16–20 = A
12–15 = B
9–11 = C
6–8 = D
0–5 = F

Research Project Grading Rubric

Name:_____ Date: _____

Resources: _____ (1-10 points)
- All required resources are present.
- Resources are appropriate for topic.

Note Cards: _____ (1-20 points)
- Correct format is used.
- No plagiarism is evident.
- Source cards are included.

Graphic Organizer and/or Outlines: _____ (1-10 points)
- Organization is present.

Research Presentation: _____ (1-30 points)
- Introduction is present.
- Research is well organized.
- Careful research is reflected.
- Conclusion is present.

Product: _____ (1-20 points)
- Product reflects research.
- Product is unique.
- Quality of product is apparent.

Bibliography: _____ (1-20 points)
- Correct format is used.

Product Unit Plan (Colonial America)

Objective: Students will learn about Colonial America.

Time Allotment for Product: 1 week

Budget for all Products: $25.00 total

Assessment: Product rubric

Product Choices: <u>Learning Styles</u>
- Verbal—news report
- Kinesthetic—rag rug
- Visual—brochure
- Technological—power point
- Auditory—audio tape

Resources:
- Books
- Magazines
- Video
- Speaker
- Computer
- Tape recorder
- Internet
- Video camera

Product Ideas

acrostic	biography	cereal box	diagram
fact file	advertisement	board game	comic strip
diary	fairy tale	animation	book
collection	display	fable	audio tape
book jacket	cinquain	drawing	flip book
art gallery	bulletin board	costume	dance
etching	brochure	booklet	chart
display	experiment	card game	children's story
dramatization	dough art	editorial	constitution
documentary	festival	folder game	filmstrip
computer animation	graph	graffiti	folklore
interview	flannel board pres.	greeting card	magazine
manual	invention	magazine article	jewelry
movie	informative speech	jingles	painting
newspaper	puppet show	mode	joke book
mural	post card	obituary	letter
lecture	learning center	newscast	poem
proposal	radio show	radio commercial	rap
report	rhyme	pop-up book	riddles
scavenger hunt	sonnet	sculpture	short story
skit	sign	poster	theory
song	table	task cards	travel poster
Venn diagram	want ad	wanted poster	TV commercial
website	trifold	trivia game	time line
travel folder	simulation	secret	billboard

Product Plan Sheet (Example)

Name: *Jane Doe*　　　　　　　**Date:** *March 15, 2010*

Product: *Game to teach about the enigma "How the Pyramids Were Built"*

Materials Required:

- *General supplies: markers, pencils, scissors, glue, and ruler*
- *Posterboard*
- *Envelopes*
- *Colored paper*
- *Self-hardening clay*
- *Box*
- *White paper*
- *Computer*

Steps Needed to Create the Product:

1. *Draw a plan for the game that includes objective of the game, directions, game pieces, card questions and appearance.*
2. *Use posterboard to draw the game board.*
3. *Put graphics and colors on the board.*
4. *Use self-hardening clay to create the game pieces.*
5. *Write or type questions on cards and cut them out.*
6. *Write or type the game objective and directions.*
7. *Put the completed game board in box with game pieces, cards, objective and directions.*
8. *Have peers play the game to test its quality.*
9. *Make any needed adjustments to the game upon recommendations of peers.*

Special Help that Might Be Needed:
I might need help from my teacher in using the computer to create graphics that will add to the appearance of my game.

Section V

Forms

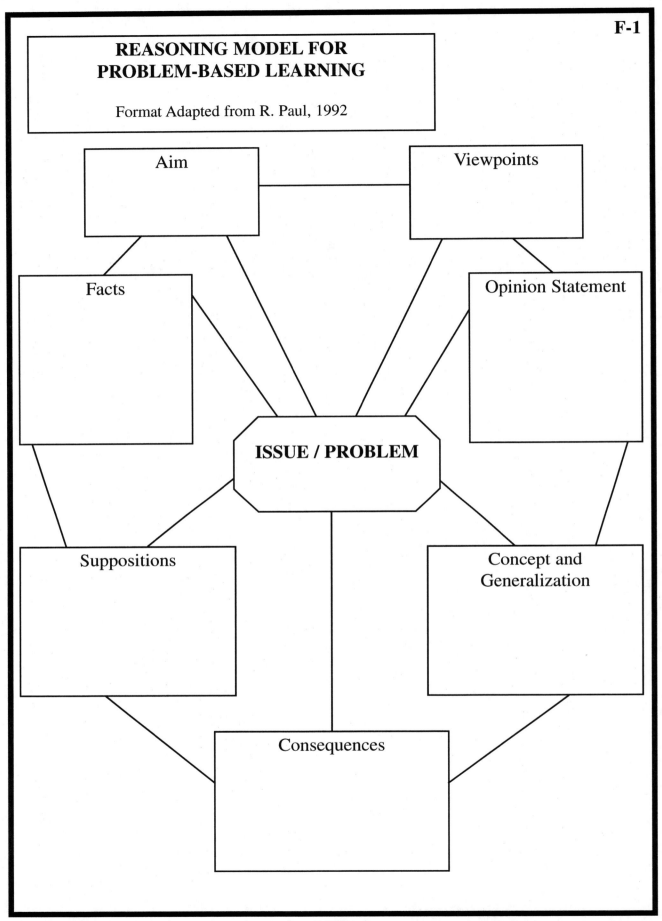

REASONING MODEL FOR PROBLEM-BASED LEARNING

Format Adapted from R. Paul, 1992

Aim

Viewpoints

Facts

Opinion Statement

ISSUE / PROBLEM

Suppositions

Concept and Generalization

Consequences

CREATIVE PROBLEM SOLVING

FACTS:

-
-
-

PROBLEM: .

IDEAS:

-
-
-
-

EVALUATION CHART:

Place a plus sign (+) under an idea for a positive evaluation and a minus sign (–) for a negative evaluation. Count the +'s and the –'s. Each + gets 3 points and each – gets 1 point. No points are allotted for no sign.

CRITERIA				

IDEA
TOTAL POINTS

NO. POSITIVE x 3 NO. NEGATIVE x -1

_____	____ x 3 = ____	____ x -1 = ____	_____
_____	____ x 3 = ____	____ x -1 = ____	_____
_____	____ x 3 = ____	____ x -1 = ____	_____
_____	____ x 3 = ____	____ x -1 = ____	_____

The idea with the most points is the possible solution to the problem.

CREATIVE PROBLEM SOLVING, continued

SOLUTION: Acceptance

What are the steps needed to solve the problem?

-
-
-
-
-
-
-
-
-
-
-

SCAMPER

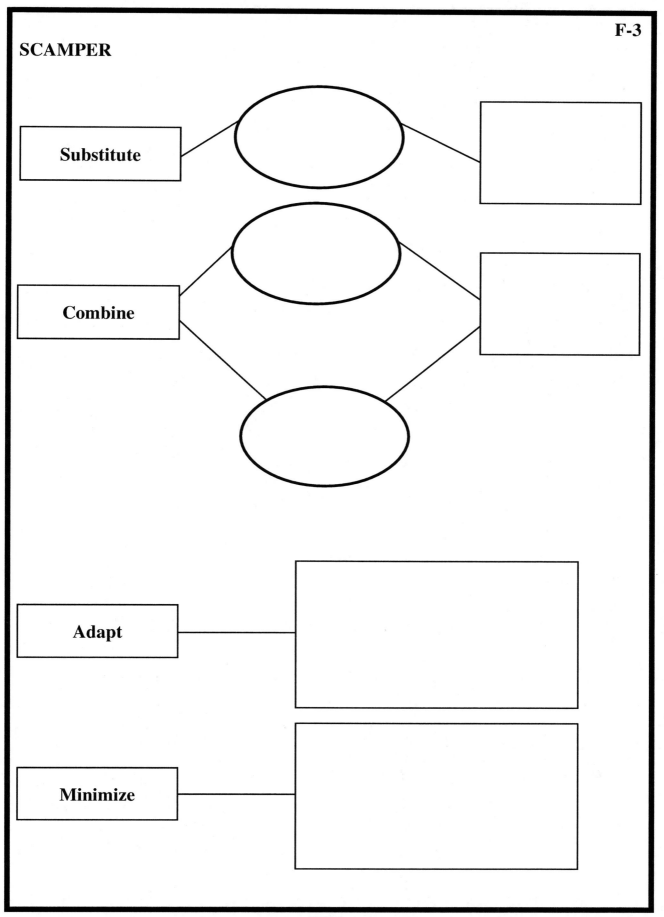

SCAMPER, continued

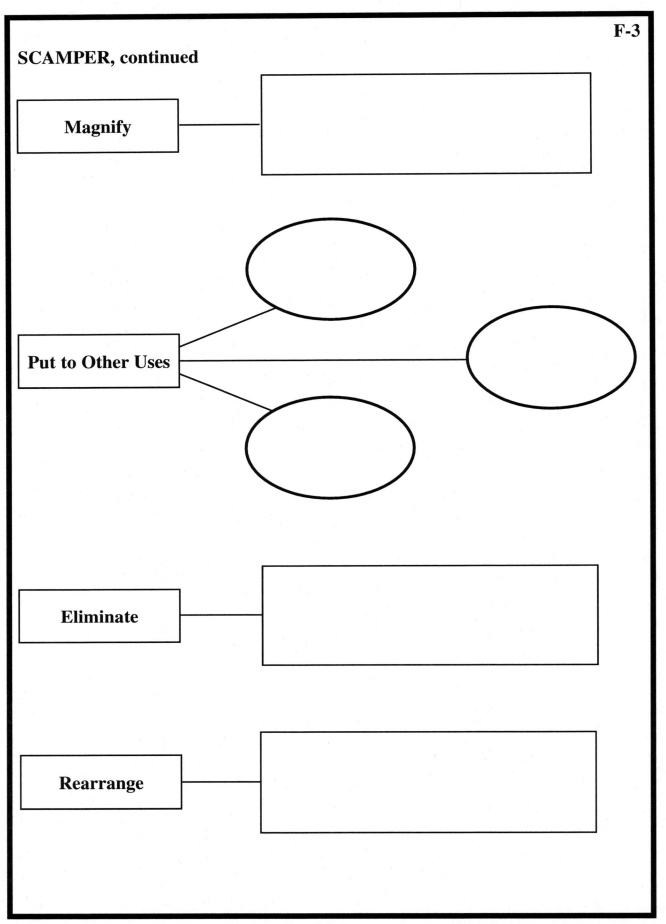

Magnify

Put to Other Uses

Eliminate

Rearrange

Interest Inventory

Name:_____ **Date:** _____

Grade: _____

1. What is your favorite subject in school? Why?

_____

_____

2. Do you like to read books? If so, what type of books do you like to read? Why?

_____

_____

3. What characteristics do you look for in a friend? Why?

_____

_____

4. What type of music do you enjoy?

_____

_____

5. If you could go on vacation anywhere in the world, where would you go? Why?

_____

_____

6 What is your favorite type of food?

_____

_____

Interest Inventory, continued

7. What is your favorite subject in school? Why?

_____

_____

8. What is your favorite T.V. show or movie?

_____

_____

9. Where do you see yourself in twenty years?

_____

_____

10. What is your favorite college that you would like to attend?

_____

_____

11. What types of activities do you enjoy?

_____

_____

12. What are your hobbies?

_____

_____

13. If you were asked to create a product for a project, what type of product would you most enjoy making?

_____

_____

Interest Inventory, continued

14. Do you have a hero? If so, who is it and why?

_____

_____

15. If you could be someone's role model, what characteristics would you like to portray?

_____

_____

16. What character traits do you dislike in people?

_____

_____

17. If you could change one thing about yourself, what would you like to change and why?

_____

_____

18. What is one thing you would like to change in the world? Why?

_____

_____

19. If you had $1,000.00, what would you do with it?

_____

_____

Learning Styles

Kinesthetic Learners...

- acquire knowledge through hands-on activities;
- enjoy using manipulatives, tools, and materials; and
- retain learning better by doing rather than listening or seeing.

Products and Performances for Kinesthetic Learners

1. Create a model of _____.

2. Design and build an invention that solves the problem of _____.

3. Create a set of manipulatives that can be used to teach _____.

4. Use a variety of art supplies to create a model of _____.

5. Design and build a set for a play about _____.

6. Create and make puppets to use in a puppet show about _____.

7. Choreograph a dance about _____ and teach it to the class.

8. Design and make a costume for a play about _____.

9. Graffiti write about _____.

10. Create a painting about _____ that can be used to teach _____.

Learning Styles

Technological Learners ...

- show an understanding of the use of technology;
- show proficiency in using technological tools such as digital cameras, video-production tools, webquest, smart boards, computers and software, etc.; and
- integrates various technology into content.

Products and Performances for Technological Learners

1. Using the computer, create a Power Point that will teach a lesson about _____.

2. Create a Power Point presentation to be used as a visual aid for _____.

3. Use clay animation to create a movie about _____.

4. Choose a core curriculum area and create a webquest that can be used to help teach a lesson about _____.

5. With the help of a smart board, create a lesson on _____.

6. Using a graphic program, create a graphic to use in a presentation about _____.

7. Use a digital camera to create graphics for a poster on the subject of _____.

8. Evaluate four websites for accuracy of information about _____.

9. Create a lesson on the computer to teach students distinguish between credible and non-credible resources for _____.

10. Using a video camera, create a movie that can be used to _____.

Learning Styles

Verbal Learners ...

- enjoy using words in both speech and writing;
- enjoy music, poetry, dialogues, skits, presentations, and taking part in debates; and
- apply verbal instructions rather than other modalities.

Products and Performances for Verbal Learners

1. Set up a debate with classmates about _____.

2. Write a poem about _____ and it to the class.

3. Create and give a news report about _____.

4. Using the lecture technique, teach a lesson about _____.

5. Conduct an interview with a classmate about _____.

6. Write and produce a radio commercial about _____.

7. Give an informative speech to the class about _____.

8. Choose a controversial subject and give your point of view about _____.

9. Create a jingle about _____ and sing it to the class.

10. Create and narrate a movie about _____.

Learning Styles

Visual Learners ...

- learn best by seeing or watching a demonstration;
- enjoy creating or looking at visual displays; and
- tend to use pictures, graphic organizers, colorful graphics, maps, story boards, etc.

Products and Performances for Visual Learners

1. Create a graph, chart, or other visual aid to use in teaching a lesson about _____.

2. Write a set of directions for an activity about _____.

3. Create and illustrate a comic strip about _____.

4. Design and illustrate a book about _____.

5. Using a set of pictures, express an idea about _____.

6. Create a painting about the idea of _____.

7. Design and illustrate a sign that can be used with _____.

8. Use a Venn diagram to compare _____ and _____.

9. Design special effects to be used in a movie about _____.

10. Create characters for a flannel board presentation about _____.

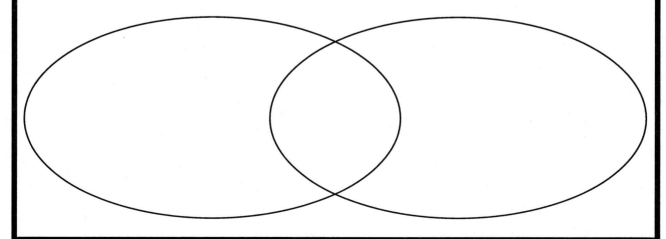

Learning Styles

Auditory Learners ...
- understand better when material is read aloud to them;
- would rather listen to music than view a piece of art work; and
- use music jingles to learn things.

Products and Performances for Auditory Learners

1. Tell a joke or story to demonstrate a point about _____.

2. Create a set of verbal instructions that can be read aloud to teach about _____.

3. Prepare an audio tape of a lesson about _____.

4. Find a song that can be used to teach a lesson about _____.

5. Create a jingle that will help the learner remember _____.

6. Design a set of oral drills that will teach about _____.

7. Create mnemonics to aid memorization of _____.

8. Tell a story to teach the concept of _____.

9. Write a poem about _____ that uses rhyme and recite it to the class.

10. Lead a discussion group on the topic of _____.

Credibility of Resources

Domain Names

.org...site: published by a non-profit organization

.com...site: published for commercial purposes

.net...site: published by a network

.edu...site: published by an educational institution

.gov...site: published by the United States government

Purpose of the Information

Discovering the reason information has been published on the Internet is sometimes tricky. Usually the purpose for .org, .com, and .net sites is to make money. One way to get an idea about the reason for publication is to check what information is being furnished and which organization is sponsoring the site. If the site seems to be a .gov or .edu site, be sure the sponsor is clearly noted.

Author of Information

Information does not always require an author, but when it does, check the author's credentials and try to determine his or her reason for publishing the article. Also, check to see if the author has included his/her e-mail address. This adds credibility to the information.

Fact or Opinion

In determining whether an article is fact or opinion, one must address several areas. These include the following:

- What resource links were used to create the article?
- Does the domain clearly state its purpose without too many advertising links?
- Is the name of the host organization present in the article?

Current Information

Regardless of how great the information is, if the link has not been updated in several years, there is a possibility that the information is outdated. Check for the following information:

- date the resource was created
- when the resource was last updated
- last date the link was checked

Credibility of Resources, continued

Linking to Other Sites

Biased information can sometimes be distinguished by checking what other websites are linked to the site. For instance, if the topic of study is the white-winged dove and other sites linked to the site include animal activists groups, then it can be concluded that the resource is probably biased against guns and hunting animals.

Richness of Information

Compare the information found in the article to the information found in data bases and other Internet sites. If the information is the same as in the data bases, this is usually a sign of the website's credibility. The information on the site should be well written and easily understood. The site should not contain grammatical or spelling errors. If several errors are found, the site should not be deemed credible.

Credibility of Internet Resources Checklist

Site Name: _____

URL: _____

Place a check beside the answer according to your observations.

	(Yes)	(No)
1. Purpose of site is clearly stated.	( )	( )
2. Name of site's author is present if applicable.	( )	( )
3. Are advertising links limited to 2?	( )	( )
4. Is the host organization's name present?	( )	( )
5. Is the date of information current (3 to 5 years)?	( )	( )
6. Has the site been updated recently (2 or 3 months)?	( )	( )
7. Are linked sites unbiased?	( )	( )
8. Is the information well written and easily understood?	( )	( )
9. Does the site's information compare to other credible resources?	( )	( )
10. Is the site free of grammatical and spelling errors.	( )	( )
TOTALS:	____	____

If you checked "Yes" to every item, you can assume the site is credible. If not, further research is needed to prove the site's credibility.

Venn diagram (2)

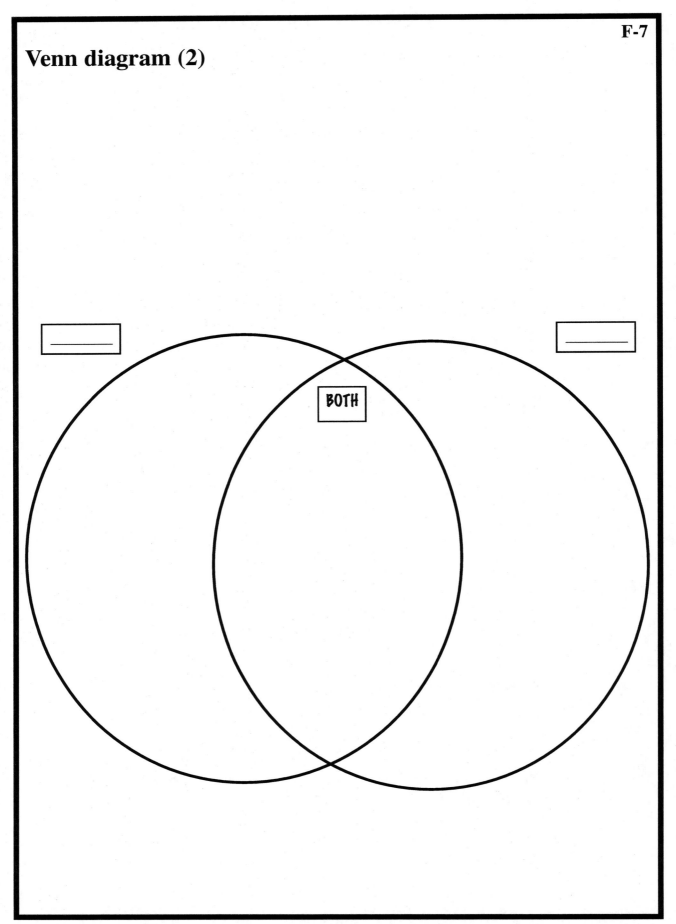

BOTH

Venn diagram (3)

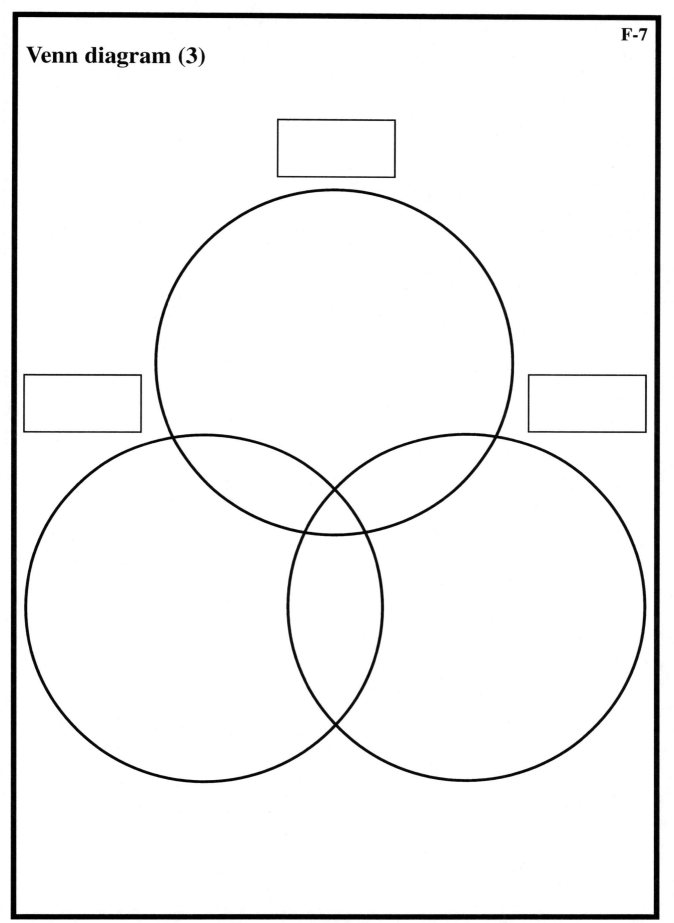

T-Chart

Sentence Frame

1. What do you know about _____?

2. I know that _____ could be used in

_____ because I learned in

_____ that _____

_____.

3. Explain another way that _____ might be used.

A _____ might be used to _____

_____ by _____

_____.

4. What might happen if the _____ did not exist?

If the _____ did not exist, then _____

_____

_____.

5. I suppose a _____ could be added to the

_____ to make a new _____

_____.

6. Other people such as _____ could use the

_____ to _____

_____

_____

_____.

Card Sort (_____)

Graphic Organizer (1)

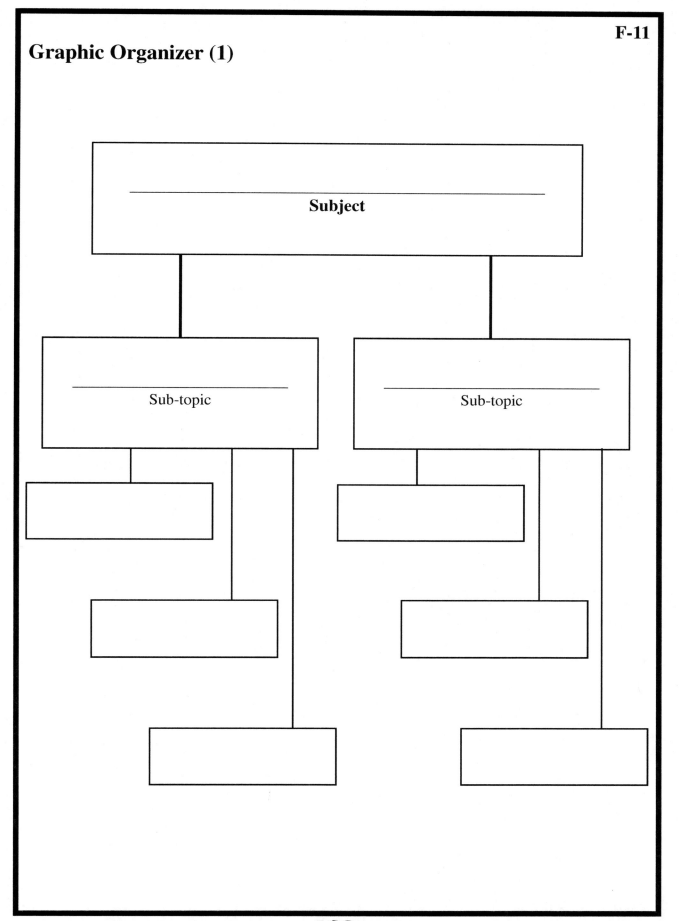

Graphic Organizer (2)

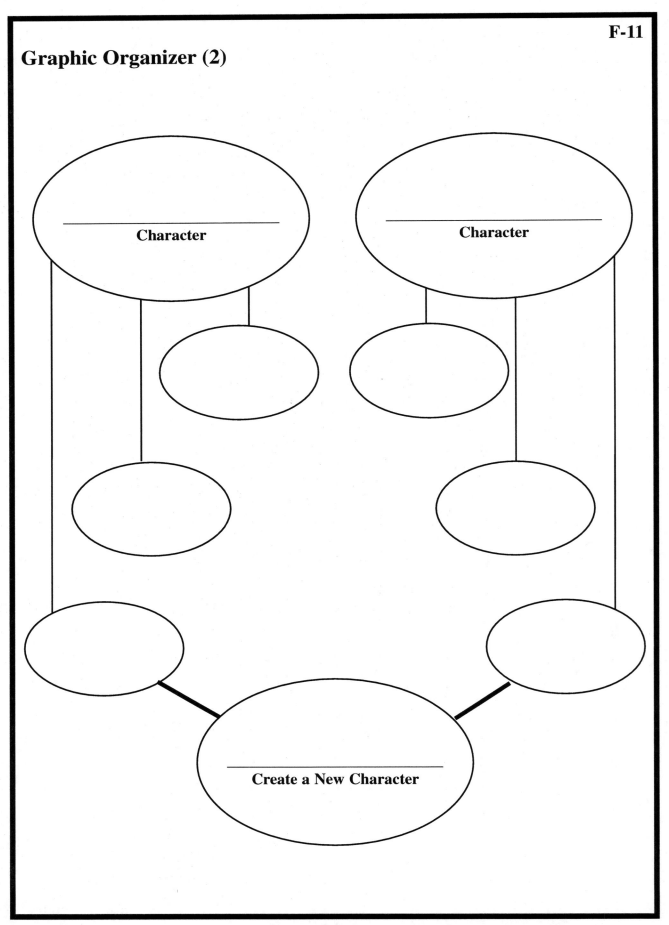

Character

Character

Create a New Character

Graphic Organizer (3)

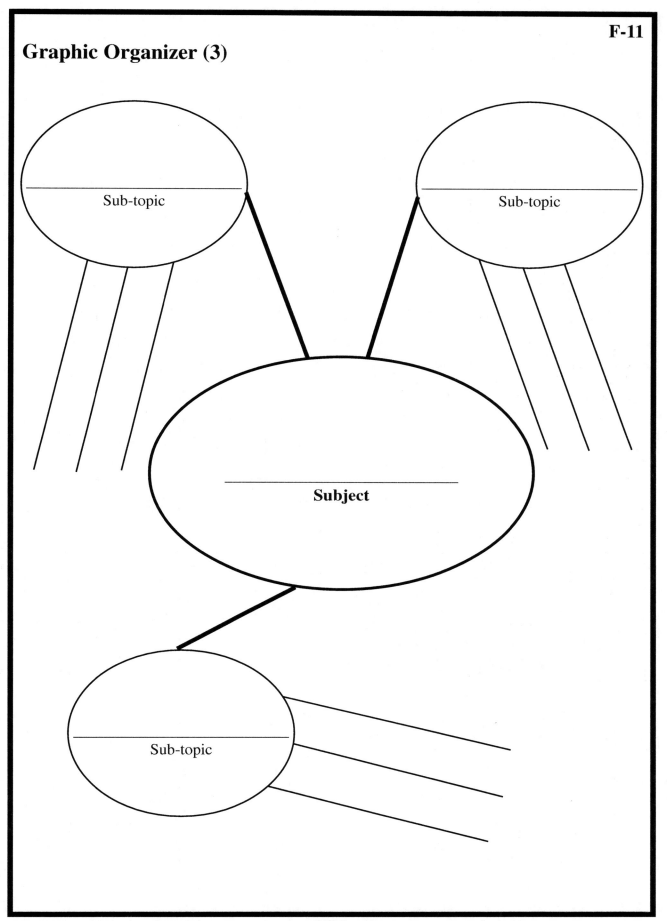

Sub-topic

Sub-topic

_____ **Subject**

Sub-topic

Concept Attainment

Design the Concept

List the Attributes

A.

B.

C.

D.

E.

Develop Positive and Negative Examples

POSITIVE	NEGATIVE
1.	1.
2.	2.
3.	3.
4.	4.
5.	5.
6.	6.
7.	7.
8.	8.
9.	9.
10.	10.

Concept Attainment, continued

Introduce the Process and Present the Examples

How:

Develop a Concept Definition

Definition:

Give More Examples if Needed

Discuss Process with Students and Evaluate Lesson

Evaluation:

Mystery Card Game (_____)

5 E's Lesson

Topic: _____

Engage:

Explore:

Explain:

Elaborate:

Evaluate:

Compacting (Grades _____)
Unit: _____ Type: _____

Demonstrated Mastery	Documentation
Standards: **Concepts and Skills:**	**Pre-assessment:**
Needs for Further Instruction	**Procedures and Resources** Date: _____ Date: _____ Date: _____
Replacement Task	**Resources**

Tiered Lesson (Grades _____)
Unit: _____

Objectives:

Whole-class Activities   **Assessment**

Level 1 Activity   **Assessment**

Level 2 Activity   **Assessment**

Level 3 Activity   **Assessment**

Whole-class Culminating Activities   **Assessment**

Student-choice Activity: _____ **Tic-Tac-Toe**
Standards/Objectives:

1.	2.	3.
4.	5.	6.
7.	8.	9.

I/we chose the following activities: No. _____, No._____, and No._____.

Name(s): _____

Due dates: _____, _____, and _____

Learning (Interest) Center Activity

Name: _____ **Subject:** _____

1.	2.	3.
4.	5.	6.
7.	8.	9.

Choose five activities and complete.

No. _____ Date completed: _____   No. _____ Date completed: _____

No. _____ Date completed: _____   No. _____ Date completed: _____

No. _____ Date completed: _____

Product Unit Plan (_____)

Objective:

Time Allotment for Product:

Budget for all Products:

Assessment:

Product Choices: Learning Styles

- Verbal—

- Kinesthetic—

- Visual—

- Technological—

- Auditory—

Resources:

Product Plan Sheet

Name: _____   **Date:** _____

Product: _____

Materials Required:

_____   _____

_____   _____

_____   _____

_____   _____

Steps Needed to Create Product:

_____

_____

_____

_____

_____

_____

_____

_____

_____

Special Help that Might Be Needed:

_____

_____

_____

_____

Product Self-reflection Sheet

Name: _____ Date: _____

Product: _____

What new information did I learn through the product creation and research?

_____

_____

_____

_____

What connections were made to other areas, if any?

_____

_____

_____

Give examples of depth and complexity that were used in my product.

_____

_____

_____

Give examples of my effort in creating this product.

_____

_____

_____

Where does my product lead me for future studies?

_____

_____

_____

Tier I Nomination Form

Date: _____

Student's Name: _____ Grade _____

Birth Date: _____ School: _____

Parent's Name & Address: _____

Is this a parent or teacher nomination? (Please place a check on the appropriate line.):

___ Parent   ___ Teacher   If Teacher, Name of Teacher: _____

Check the characteristics student exhibits most of the time during class.

___ Uses vocabulary above grade level

___ Understands numerical concepts beyond age expectations

___ Has insight and readily grasps the intent and directions of ideas

___ Drawing may be sophisticated, elaborate for age level

___ Shows originality in expression (verbal and written)

___ Is a self-motivated learner, enjoys learning.

___ Possesses high standards of performance for self

___ Senses a deeper meaning to an answer by producing more detailed steps

___ Reveals originality in ideas

___ Has unusual sensitivity to people's feelings

___ Has answers to questions most of the time

___ Perseveres in problem solving work

___ Works well in groups

___ Has a well developed sense of humor

___ Is task committed (completes tasks promptly)

___ Can read above age expectations

___ Is a keen and alert observer

___ Masters the basic skills quickly

___ Displays an unusual curiosity

___ Masters the basic skills quickly

___ Transfers learning easily (generalizes)

___ Organizes and uses time wisely

___ Works well independently

___ Handles social situations easily

___ Is accepted by classmates

___ Has high energy level

___ Fantasizes, imagines, manipulates

___ Has a positive attitude

___ Has ability to organize people

___ Is an independent thinker

Tier I Nomination Form, page 2   **Date:** _____

Student's Name: _____   Grade _____

Measures Used for Testing (Achievement, IQ, Creativity, Product Portfolios, Motivational Scales, Teacher, Parent, and/or Student Interviews)

Measure	Date	Score
_____	_____	_____
_____	_____	_____
_____	_____	_____
_____	_____	_____
_____	_____	_____
_____	_____	_____

Area/s of Giftedness, if known: _____

Other comments or information:

_____

_____

_____

_____

_____

Does the student meet the criteria for the Gifted and Talented Program: ___ Yes   ___ No

Date: _____

Committee Signatures

_____

_____

_____

_____

_____

Tiers II and III Nomination Form

Date: _____

Student's Name: _____

Grade Placed in Gifted Program: _____

Area of Giftedness, if Known: _____

Topic of Study: _____

Teacher Providing Services: _____

Check the intervention strategies to be used with the student.

Best Practices for Differentiation

____ Critical Thinking   ____ Creative Thinking

____ Depth and Complexity   ____ Concept-based Learning

____ Research and Independent Study   ____ Other: _____

Research-based Strategies

____ Identifying Similarities & Differences   ____ Nonlinguistic Representations

    ____ Venn Diagram   ____ Graphic Organizers

    ____ T-Chart   ____ Kinesthetic

    ____ Sentence Frames   ____ Role Play

    ____ Card Sort   ____ Demonstrations, Models, Illustrations, Pictographs

____ Cooperative Learning   ____ Generating & Testing Hypothesis

    ____ Think-Pair Share   ____ Concept Attainment

    ____ Fact-or-Fiction   ____ Deductive/Inductive Thinking

    ____ Toss-a-Question   ____ Mystery Concept

    ____ Stand and Share   ____ 5 E's Lesson

    ____ Find Someone Who:

        ____ Other: _____

Tiers II and III Nomination Form, page 2   Date: _____

Name: _____

Classroom Management Strategies

___ Curriculum Compacting   ___ Tiered Assignments

___ Interest Centers/Groups   ___ Learning Stations

___ Agenda   ___ Exit Cards

___ Learning Contracts   ___ Other: _____

Independent Research Project with Product

___ Research Project with Product and Presentation

Topic: _____

Student's Area(s) of Interest

_____   _____

_____   _____

_____   _____

_____   _____

Student's Learning Style (Check appropriate area.)

____ **Visual**   ____ **Kinesthetic**   ____ **Technological**   ____ **Verbal**   ____ **Auditory**

Notes on Student

_____

_____

_____

_____

_____

_____

Bibliography

BOOKS

Brophy, Jere & Thomas L. Good. *Handbook of Research on Teaching.* New York: Macmillan, 1986.

Carlile, Vowery. *Ready to Research...Animals.* Hawthorne, NJ: Educational Impressions, 2005.

—— *Ready to Research....Famous People.* Hawthorne, NJ: Educational Impressions, 2006.

—— *Creative Experiences in Science: Insects.* Hawthorne, NJ: Educational Impressions, 2008.

—— *Creative Experiences in Science: The Earth.* Hawthorne, NJ: Educational Impressions, 2009.

—— *Enigmas.* Hawthorne, NJ: Educational Impressions, 2009.

Carlile, Vowery & Traci Burnett. *A Creative Look at Texas History for Middle School Students.* Hawthorne, NJ: Educational Impressions, 2008.

—— *Creative Experiences in U.S. History.* Hawthorne, NJ: Educational Impressions, 2009.

Casbarro, Joseph. *RTI-Response-To-Intervention.* Port Chester, NY: National Professional Resources, Inc., 2008.

Coil, Carolyn. *Encouraging Achievement.* Dayton, OH: Pieces of Learning, 1999.

—— *Standards-Based Activities and Assessments for the Differentiated Classroom.* Marion, IL.: Pieces of Learning, 2004.

—— *Successful Teaching in the Differentiated Classroom.* Marion, IL.: Pieces of Learning, 2006.

Coleman, J.S., E. Campbell, C. Hobson, J. McPartland, A. Mood, F. Weinfeld, and R. York. *Equality of Educational Opportunity.* Washington, DC: U.S. Government Printing Office, 1966.

Decker, Tressa and Kay Davidson. *Bloom's and Beyond: Higher Level Questions and Activities for the Creative Classroom.* Marion, IL.: Pieces of Learning, 2006.

Doherty, Barbara and Charlotte Jaffe. *Differentiated Instruction, Grades 3 to 6: Language Arts.* Hawthorne, NJ: Educational Impressions, 2008.

—— *Differentiated Instruction, Grades 3 to 6: Science.* Hawthorne, NJ: Educational Impressions, 2008.

—— *Differentiated Instruction, Grades 3 to 6: Social Studies.* Hawthorne, NJ: Educational Impressions, 2008.

Gentner, Dedre and Arthur .B. Markman. "Structural Alignment in Comparison: No difference without Similarity." *Psychological Science,* 5(3), 1994.

Harken, Shannon. Professional Learning and Leadership Consultant, Heartland AEA 11. sharken@aea11.k12.ia.us

Heacox, Diane. *Differentiating Instruction in the Regular Classroom.* Minneapolis, MN: Free Spirit Publishing Inc., 2002.

Johnson, Nancy. *Active Questioning.* Dayton, OH: Pieces of Learning, 1995.

Kagan, Spencer. *Cooperative Learning.* San Juan Capistrano, CA: Kagan Cooperative Learning, 1992.

Kaplan, S.N. *Inservice Training Manual: Activities for Developing Curriculum for the Gifted and Talented.* Los Angeles: National/State Leadership Training Institute on the Gifted and Talented, 1979.

Kingore, Bertie. *Differentiation: Simplified, Realistic, and Effective.* Austin, Tx.: Professional Associates Publishing, 2004.

Marzano, Robert J., Debra J. Pickering, and Jane E. Pollock. *Classroom Instruction that Works.* Alexandria, Virginia: Association for Supervision and Curriculum Development, 2001.

Mayfield, Missy and Shelby Waller. *Connecting the Pieces of the RTI Puzzle.* Wichita Falls, TX: Region IX ESC, 2008.

Medin, D., R.LO. Goldstone, and A.B. Markman. "Comparison and Choice: Relations between Similarity Processes and Decisions Process." *Psychonomic Bulletin & Review,* 2 (1), 1996.

Merritt, Dodie. *Independent Study Where Creative Minds Expand.* Dayton, OH: Pieces of Learning, 2001.

Michalko, Michael. *Thinkertoys: A Handbook of Creative-Thinking Techniques.* Berkeley, CA: Ten Speed Press, 2006.

No Child Left Behind Act, Texas Education Agency, 2004

Parnes, Sidney J. *Source Book for Creative Problem Solving.* Buffalo: Creative Foundation Press, 1992.

Reis, Sally M., Burns, D. E., and Renzulli, J. S. *Curriculum Compacting: The Complete Guide to Modifying the Regular Curriculum for High-ability Students.* Mansfield Center, CT: Creative Learning Press, 1992.

Renzulli, Joseph S., & Smith, L. H. *The Compactor.* Mansfield Center, CT: Creative Learning Press, 1978.

Sanders, William L. & Sandra P. Horn. "The Tennessee Value-added Assessment System (TVAAS): Mixed-model Methodology in Educational Assessment." *Journal of Personnel Press,* 1992.

Starko, Alane J. *It's About Time.* Mansfield Center, CT: Creative Learning Press, Inc., 1986.

Tomlinson, Carol. *The Differentiated Classroom, Responding to the Needs of All Learners.* Alexandria, VA: Association for Supervision and Curriculum Development, (ASCD), 1999.

——· *Fulfilling the Promise of the Differentiated Classroom.* Alexandria, VA: Association for Supervision and Curriculum Development, (ASCD), 2003.

Witherell, Nancy L. and Mary C. McMackin. *Graphic Organizers and Activities for Differentiated Instruction in Reading.* New York, NY: Scholastic, 2002.

ELECTRONIC RESOURCES

"Best Practices: Instructional Strategies and Techniques" October 20, 2009
http://www.saskschools.ca/curr_content/bestpractice/tiered/index.html
http://wblrd.sk.ca/~bestpractice/tiered/assessment.html

"Critical Thinking" October 20, 2009. www.edhelper.com/critical_thinking.htm.

"Problem Solving" November 14, 2009. http://www.gdrc.org/decision/problem-solve.html"

S-CA-M-P-E-R" 11-15-2009. http://litemind.com/scamper/

"Texas Performance Standards Project" September 10, 2009. www.texaspsp.org

"Tiered Curriculum Project" November 10, 2009
http://www.doe.state.in.us/exceptional/gt/tiered_curriculum/welcome.html

"Tiered Lesson Plans" November 10, 2009. http://www.manhattan.k12.ca.us/staff/pware/diff/

Website Resources

Section I

Interest Inventories
http://printables.scholastic.com/printables/detail/?id=35571
http://www.sanchezclass.com/docs/student-interest-inventory.pdf
http://www.saskschools.ca/curr_content/adapthandbook/learner/interest.html
http://www.cdrcp.com/Transitions%20page%20PDF/Student%20Interests.pdf

Learning Modalities
http://www.saskschools.ca/curr_content/adapthandbook/learner/l_style.html

The learning styles inventories below can be taken online, submitted and the modality given within a few minutes.
http://www.engr.ncsu.edu/learningstyles/ilsweb.html
http://www.ldpride.net/learning-style-test.html
http://people.usd.edu/~bwjames/tut/learning-style/stylest.html

Resource Credibility
http://www.tammypayton.net/courses/search/credible2.shtml

Section II

Venn Diagram
http://www.readwritethink.org/materials/venn/
http://www.2learn.ca/construct/graphicorg/venn/vennindex.html
http://www.enchantedlearning.com/graphicorganizers/venn/

T-Chart
http://www.worksheetworks.com/miscellanea/graphic-organizers/tchart.html

Non-Linguistic
http://edweb.tusd.k12.az.us/Templates/nonlinguisticrepresentations.htm

Concept Attainment
http://olc.spsd.sk.ca/DE/PD/instr/strats/cattain/

Inductive/Deductive Thinking
http://www.nakedscience.org/mrg/Deductive%20and%20Inductive%20Reasoning.htm

Notes